I0413871

REDISCOVER <small>YOUR</small>
UNIQUE
TIMELESS
VALUE

REDISCOVER YOUR UNIQUE TIMELESS VALUE

REDISCOVERING THE **PURPOSE, PRIORITY,** AND **POWER** OF **KINGDOM VALUES** THAT INFLUENCE **MY PERSONAL LIFE**

AUDIE CASIGURAN

PARTRIDGE

Copyright © 2017 by Audie Casiguran.

ISBN: Softcover   978-1-5437-4340-1
                 eBook   978-1-5437-4341-8

All rights reserved. No part of this book may be used or reproduced by any means, graphic, electronic, or mechanical, including photocopying, recording, taping or by any information storage retrieval system without the written permission of the author except in the case of brief quotations embodied in critical articles and reviews.

Because of the dynamic nature of the Internet, any web addresses or links contained in this book may have changed since publication and may no longer be valid. The views expressed in this work are solely those of the author and do not necessarily reflect the views of the publisher, and the publisher hereby disclaims any responsibility for them.

Unless otherwise indicated, all Scripture quotations are from the Holy Bible, New International Version®, (NIV), © 1973, 1978, 1984 by the International Bible Society. Used by permission of Zondervan. All rights reserve. Scripture quotations marked (NKJV) are from the New King James Version, © 1979, 1980, 1982, 1984 by Thomas Nelson, Inc. Used by permission. All right reserved. Scripture quotations marked (KJV) are taken from the King James Version of the Holy Bible Scripture.

Print information available on the last page.

To order additional copies of this book, contact
Toll Free 800 101 2657 (Singapore)
Toll Free 1 800 81 7340 (Malaysia)
orders.singapore@partridgepublishing.com

www.partridgepublishing.com/singapore

CONTENTS

DEDICATION

For all of my peers in YMCO KSA, GPL families,
and to all of my friends, this book is for you.

This also dedicated to my Father Jesse Z. Casiguran
and my Mother Maribel F. Casiguran, and my
siblings; Jesse II and Michelle Marie Casiguran

To my wife Susan Puyo Casiguran, thank you for
your patience and trust and also thank you to the
lives of my children's E.J. and Princess.

Last but not the least, to my Chief Cornerstone, my King of Kings
and Lord of Lords of my life - Eshua (Jesus) Meshika (Messiah),
Honor and glory and dominion is your forever and ever,

Thy Kingdom come and thy will be done. Amen!

*"I say to you, unless a grain of wheat falls into the ground
and dies, it remains alone; but if it dies,
it produces much grain."*

(Book of John XII:XXIV, NKJV)

PREFACE

E verything has to be started in an Idea; this book was written in order that I must left these ideas on paper. Ideas outlived men, all of these written ideas I believed is needed by our generation and the next generation to come and somebody has to write this content; to document the ideas. The whole book deals on two main single ideas. "Kingdom" and "Values". This Ideas isn't new anymore but it is only a recombination of old ideas in my own perspective way. This book will help them to learn how to be, "become a person of value". I have a dream that this book will connect somehow, The Source (God) and you to influence, inspired and motivate people to look for themselves their true human value and dignity in the eyes of the Creator that they might have a sense of purpose, meaning, and significance on this life, and not only paying mortgage, bills, and die.

I believe that every person was born to be significant: I am one of the many voices to help other people to think they can and find their "Author/Manufacturer" purpose in life which will cause them to acknowledge the Source and follow their destiny.

I dreamed that everyone finds their own gift to influence other people to Honor God, in discovering their true value which will cause to improve others, pursue their dreams, produce great people, speak the value of human dignity, understanding that our life is full of potential, our life is valuable, our life is significant to others, and so fulfilling the purpose of transferring our right human values to the next generation; this is the reason why the book was created.

This book was also a result of my personal struggle, not knowing my self-identity, my self-concept of worth, how much valuable my life is, I have seen that many of my country-men and all of the Third world nations, have poor self-mentality by their own mind that their life is relegated only to the bottom of the society, nation, and country. I hate when I saw people who are oppressed, suppressed, and depressed by the pattern of our culture, "superiority and inferiority ideas" developed by the history of men. I am convinced that every person is born to be great valued but because of the cultural-mindset, society influence, family up-bringing, religion background, and of the world system, they tend to believe that they are just sub-ordinary person (less than a human value); first exist in their minds and reflected through their actions and personal life.

I see that, this book will serve only as one of many voices who are telling others and about you that your life is valuable, significant, and full-of-meaning. You do not need to imitate any other person in this world because, I see every person is unique and wonderfully crafted, design, produced by the divine manufacturer, and has an infinite value of His Image on him and her.

May this book serve you and help you find your self-value, purpose and vision of your life through the message of the King. "King Eshua" (King Jesus) in his teaching about the "Kingdom of God".

PROLOGUE

The value of a man should be seen in what he gives
and not in what he is able to receive.

Albert Einstein

Human needs

There are 7.3 billion people around the world according to the United States Census Bureau since the year of 2017.One birth for every 8 seconds; one death for every 12 seconds; and one International migrant (net) for every 32 seconds. And our global populations are still increasing, since the dawn of our human civilization and human flourishing from the foundation of the world.

Human needs are constantly motivated by any means of survival starting from physiological needs such as i.e. food, water, and shelter. Next, psychological needs such as i.e. intimate relationship, family, friends, esteem needs such as i.e. prestige, feeling accomplishment, and lastly the needs of Self-Actualization which means to achieve one's potential, including creative activities to produce meaning, and sense of purpose and destiny.

It seems that in all of that 7.3 billon people over the world, there are all motivated in just two most common needs of a human being; self-preservation and human security. Therefore, every human on the planet earth needs the self-preservation and human security. Human will always value what preserved him and secured his generation, whether you lived inside a mansion or the beggar under-the-bridge, whether you are living an American dream life of living inside the jungle of South America, whether you are Ph.D. Emeritus degree in an Ivy-league school universities or no-read-no-write at all, no matter what's the color of your pigmentation; black, white, yellow, brown, whether you are part of an Aristocrat family or an orphanage, we have the same needs. Thus, we will always value our self-preservation and our security.

According to one of well-known American psychologist in the 21st century, his name was Abraham Maslow, his extensive research on human motivational needs gives him the most famous subject, "Maslow's hierarchy of needs" proposed on 1943 paper, entitled: "A Theory of Human Motivation". Based on his extensive research stated above, all humans will always and constantly value the basic needs and we are motivated to seek, pursue, run-to, all these things in order to preserved and secure our human value.

What does it mean to be a human? (This is only a rhetorical question), Is there any value to be a human in this era? It doesn't matter where you are right now in this world or what statuses you've accomplished have in life, whether you are celebrity or an outcast people, every human being will always seek these two primarily things.

They need all that things to conserve human. From the time of Hellenistic Greek ideas, to the Roman Empire which brought all of these ideas and spread around the world, that man (human-kind-species) is searching for a better country or better government in order to get all of those needs mention by Maslow's hierarchy. That all of us, including me are looking and searching for a better country and or of good government which will provide our *Two* primary needs in order to preserved and secured humanity.

Now, all of us need food, water, shelter, family-relationship, friends, prestige & accomplishments, meaning and ultimately purpose in life. These needs established in us in order for us to function by and all of us seek these things, in order, to fill our lives with meaning. We normally tend to seek success, in order to receive; one is pleasure, second is power, and third is meaning in our human entire lives.

I've never met a person who doesn't want to be success, everyone wants to be success from an age of seven-year-old child to a seventy years old adult man, and everyone wants to be success. Our successes are defined by those things mention above. The human hunger problem is that we are looking for our legitimate needs to an illegitimate source, by means of taking-shortcuts. We focus our value on things that fulfill our basic needs and yet we violate some natural and divine principles in the midst of process to achieve.

In the times of Emperor Tiberius Caesar, where the glorious Roman Empire ruled the known western world, there was one small village colonized by Romans, is called Nazareth, Galilee. There was a man named Eshua (Hebrew/Aramaic), Isah (Arabic), or Jesus (Greek/ English), a simple teacher, He's statement was radical from his time and until this present age.

> He says, "Do not worry about your life, what you will *eat*, what you will *drink*, what you will *wear*, is not life more than food, and the body more than clothes? Watch now, He doesn't say it is bad to have these things; our body needs it, not wants these things. (See Book of Matthew chapter VI, article XXV NIV), and also, it is mention in one of ancient book of Isaiah that, "Come, all you are *thirsty*, come to the waters; and you have no money, come, buy and *eat!* Come, buy *wine* and *milk* without money

> and without cost (emphasis added, see Book of
> Isaiah chapter LV, article I NIV)

Notice, He does not cancel our physical (eat, drink, and wear) basic needs. If you carefully reading his statements, it's all legitimate needs, He said, and He understands it, as part of human being, Yet, the only differ from our human psychologist, behavioral scientist, Ph.D. professor, and other horizontally human philosophy concept is that; we need to have a paradigm shift of focus of *values* from seeking first our basic needs as first priority into much more valuable which our "Self-Actualization", or "Self-realization, or "Self-concept", or "Self-value, and or Self-meaning. i.e. God-given-purpose. What do I mean, Jesus tends to up-side down the Maslow's hierarchy of needs, instead of seeking first food and water, he makes unusual statements that, we need first to seek the *Self-actualization.*

He meant, the five simple questions in our human heart; that we keep ignoring because of our busy-ness and cultural-trained environment. Where we came from? The question of our Source or heritage; Who Am I? The question of our True Identity; Why I am here? The question of purpose and meaning, which is our deep true assignment; and Where will I go after this life? The question of destiny or destination in the future.

If you are carefully reading again the book of Matthew 6:25 until it reaches his conclusion in verse 33, which he defines the Two most important priorities of human are to seek first His country called "The Kingdom of heaven" and "being in-right-position" to his kingdom Government.

The final solution in which his best offers to our inner most problem and crisis, in which we fall out-of-position. I quote King Jesus, *"But seek first his Kingdom and his Righteousness, and all these things will be given to you as well"* (see. Matthew 6:33 NIV)

What he meant by that, I said earlier that we are all looking for better country or good governance, so that, all of our needs will be met. That's why, we have many migrants happening around the world, and this is the main government problem in so many countries about the issue of illegal immigrants, everyone is looking for a better country and / or good government.

Where is the opportunity, to seek better life, to be personal success in all aspect of our lives including first our family, career-job, relationships, and being self-fulfill; All of these can be found only inside a country or good government and not in *religion*, whether from the time of our early human civilization to our modern technological advance-internet-one-world based, we are always finding and travelling, looking for a better country. Even to a song sung by John Lennon, called "Imagine" were his lyrics says, *"Imagine there's no countries* (why countries? Because all are fighting for their basic needs searching for better country) *It isn't hard to do, nothing to kill or die for and no religion too* (notice he mention religion, did you know that, religion is the first reason why people hate each other and religion creates more human problem rather than solving it), *imagine all the people living life in peace"* (emphasis added in parenthesis).

Kingdom country & gov't of Heaven

Did you know that, King Eshua (Jesus) had no different idea than the same solution from us which is to seek, our long-time human crisis, to shift our human focus on the most important things in life, to Value, First the purpose he has prepared in us before the beginning of time, is to seek first his better country, which is the Heaven's government country influences our personal lives, and our environment, and circumstances. Thus, it produced a by-product of satisfaction that all that things needed are met inside in his *"invisible"* but *"real"* country.

His country is more real than us, His country constitution says, "The seen was made by the things unseen..." (Paraphrased; see. Book of Hebrew 11:3 NIV)

And, "The seen is temporal but the things unseen is eternal" (paraphrased; see. Book of II Corinthians 4:18 NIV), Therefore, His country is more durable and forever and ever established than our so-called "first-world-countries", I mean the advance Industrious nation in the world.

King Eshua, does not cancel nor denied our human insatiable needs (*not wants*). He just corrects our priorities (First-things-first) of our core-values. To shift our focus to His "Kingdom-country mind-set", that is why, it is called the good-news.

I quote from an ancient book, what is the King will bring into this world.

> "Of the greatness of His *government* and *peace* there will be no end. He (King Eshua or Jesus the Christ) will reign on (king) David's throne and over His Kingdom (country), establishing and upholding it with justice and righteousness (righteous means right-positioning-with-the-government)   from that time on and forever". (Emphasis added by parenthesis; see Book Isaiah chapter IX, article VII NIV).

He brings his government on planet earth because in his country, there's no crisis, sickness, disease, wars, poverty, oppression, and lastly death, which are why it is called, the good-message. It is so good that his Kingdom country provides a right government with his citizen – a solution to our endless human violence, crimes, wars, terrorism, and in-short to our human security needs.

From his perspective, if we tend to value his good-message about the "Kingdom of God influence", we will not be experiencing what we are right now, but we will truly have experience a real transformation, first in our minds, by renewing our mind with his own message which will later affect our lifestyle, moral, culture, and, personal values. We will see and taste that the Lord's purpose (Will) is good, pleasing, and, perfect.

Right in this moment, people all around the globe experienced negative effects of our human value crisis. We have many cultural-clashes because of many people are travelling in-and-out-of-the-countries and settling their entire families into another country, to survive, and or to flourish, looking for a better government which will provide all of their basic needs.

INTRODUCTION

"Success does not pursue, it must be ensued"

Late Dr. Viktor E. Frankl

My Personal Background Story

To begin reading this book, I must inform you also that, in every manuscript there always be a personal background story behind the writer's motive, why the book was wrote and his pre-conception ideas before this work-of-art takes place.

First let me introduce you to myself, I am the eldest son of Mr. Jesse Zacate Casiguran and Mrs. Maribel Bernaldo Francisco. With three siblings, my nick-name was "dek". I was born in Sampaloc, Manila, Philippines. We lived travelling from one place to another since my childhood. We only stayed long for two years maximum and then transferring again to another place, until such time, we permanently arrived in the Visayas region of the Philippines, in the Island of Samar. There I stayed for almost a decade.

My parent enrolled me in a private catholic boys high-school, called Christ-the-King College. All of the school directors were related from Franciscan missionaries, in that school, I learned all the catholic beliefs, doctrines, and catechism. As I grow as teen-ager, I was only interested into three main activities; listen to rock-genre music (like i.e. matchbox 20), played table-tennis (ping-pong), and reading astronomy or watching the stars at night-sky.

I was growing uninterested mainly in Christian religion, rituals, tradition, and so-called spiritual things, but in the opposite spectrum, I was insatiable, avid, science-student, and learner.

I believed there were only material world and no spirits "unseen" world. If I can still remember, I was going to a secret transition of my personal belief. starting from an Agnostic point-of-view (mean, I was not sure if there was a divine being, called *"Elohim"* and if it is possible to know him, maybe there was no time for me, to understand him, and got all-the-evidence), into the next philosophy (philosophy means the thoughts I love to think), which is a Naturalistic, atheistic, material, scientific-worldview (which means I believe only the universe exist, no spirits, no miracle, only science leads to truth, and also, it renders no restrain from my guilt from any moral restriction coming from a divine-being commandments, and thus, I can lived whatever I want it should be.)

After high-school, I went to college, finished a Five-year course degree in BSc. in Electrical engineering. All I dreamt that time was to find a job suitable for me, my skills, to help my parent and my two siblings, to finance their school tuition fee and other financial responsibilities in the family, in-short to become the "bread-winner-of-the-family" (means I was the resource of the family's income).

Everything was okay that time, as I though it should be. From my personal perspective, everything was achievable by hard-work, diligent, and being inquisitive all the time. Suddenly, I got a surprised open-opportunity working in the country of Kingdom of Saudi Arabia or KSA. Initially I thought that, I was only special lucky person, but later soon I've realized that, it was a part of an over-arch, pre-destined, purpose in my life.

The moment I received the working-visa from KSA, that season, before the job-offer abroad, I personally resign from my previous job as a permanent employee, technical support from a local construction-firm company. That time, was in the year of 2009 where the economy of the Philippines and other Asian countries were starting to melt because of global financial crisis in the West.

Working for almost three years and suddenly without any second-thought and personal plan, and financial savings, I dumped my job foolishly without reconsideration that I was the bread-winner of the family and careful thought about the job-market inside the country of Philippines.

In spite of my ignorance, what serious crisis I put myself into, because of my careless decision, lack of wisdom and poor future-planning. Suddenly, I received a phone-call from a man-power agency – not just an ordinary phone-call but a good message phone-call, that I have received a job-order and interview with my new employer. Without any clue as I grasped what was really happened to that day, I thought to myself, it was like a Miracle. Miracle because I've never went to any one, to any job-hiring conference, to any agency, nor any company for any job interview.

As to how they've find me, later the agency told me that they've search and find my resume in the internet-site. As far as I've remember, I placed my curriculum-vitae in the year 2006, for three years had pass-by, that time, I already forgot it, just because it was long-time and I've never expect it will have a chance to be chosen in a million.

The probability of finding my resume in the season of my personal decision after resignation and three years from the time I place my cv was to me a rare case of opportunity, therefore, with hesitation, I reply to the agency, check the next day and saw the website of the agency, if they are legitimate, and then I start the processed. Passing through the process was not so easy, but with little faith and wide vision I have, I begin to take risk, and went back every morning to the job again, then start over again for the process such as medical check-up, test, etc., in addition also, to pay extra for our working visa. I borrowed money and later I pay it back with my salary.

One moment, I remember that in the midst of that processing, there was a time that I've spent all of my money completely, as in totally zero money while I was on the processing of my papers going to the manpower agency. I am deeply in gratitude to one of my peer engineer, forgot her name, but without her little financial assistance, maybe I will not be here.

Two months pass-by, I completed all the necessary requirements together with the required payment, I arrived in KSA on October, 16th of 2009. From this time forward, everything was history.

As I arrived in KSA, months and years pass-by, working and working, day and night, send monthly remittances to the Philippines, work and work again, I became familiar with the routine of being an overseas worker for years. Then suddenly, despite of my personal success with my job-career and family bread-winner (in my own perspective and subjective experience only), I became to feel the sense of dullness deep inside of me.

I arrived in a stage of my personal life, where I asked myself, *"What's next?"*, *"Is there anything I can do that will bring self-fulfillment?"* In reality, in spite of a well-paid job, I felt empty, even if, I can buy whatever I want, attend some religious Christian organization, went to ministry, and serve people, then work again from Saturday to Thursday in the company (In Kingdom of Saudi Arabia, the holidays are Friday and Saturday for your information because they used lunar calendar instead of western calendar). It's more like, the more I gain

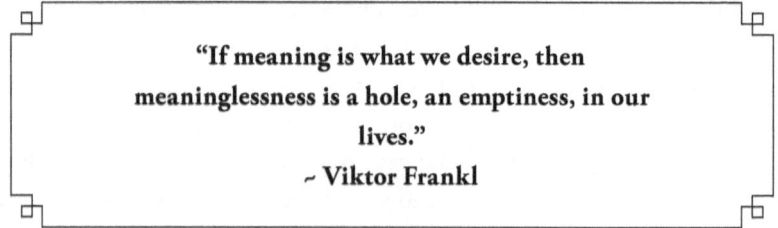

> "If meaning is what we desire, then meaninglessness is a hole, an emptiness, in our lives."
> ~ Viktor Frankl

in this world, or perceived by others that I had something, still deep-inside of me, I felt unfulfilled.

Little Psychological disclosure

One of the eminent disciple of Sigmund Freud and influenced by Alfred Adler, was the name, Mr. Viktor E. Frankl, a Neurologist and Psychiatrist at the same time, also a Holocaust survivor in the II World war. He called this stage-of-mine as, *"Existential vacuum"*.

Existential vacuum according to him was simply means, "If meaning is what we desire, then meaninglessness is a "hole", emptiness, in our lives." Whenever you have a vacuum, of course, things rush in to fill it. Frankl suggests that one of the most conspicuous signs of existential vacuum in our society was *"Boredom"*.

As he suggests, I was in this state of boredom in my personal life, where all of my so-called personal success, accolades, achievements, and rituals (without comparing to others) was nothing and did not bring joy inside of me. I am still dissatisfied, I thought that, the ultimate pursuit of life was to seek or pursue happiness / pleasure.

As the American constitution was coined the phrase, "The pursuit of happiness..." as pursuit of happiness is my personal deep-concern, by any means of pleasure, I can squeeze out-of-this-life, that was my deep motivational force. The more personal pleasure I received the more I am motivated, but this was not true in my life. Paradoxically, the more pleasure I received the more emptiness I had. (I speak only for my own self-point-of-view).

As many others don't know, including my inner family, I was plaque by uncontrollable, deadly-habit, addicted to porn, and self-depression. It was a long-time deadly habit but it was never serious enough as I thought it before, but now, As I thought to myself, if this my secret addiction will never stop, soon I realized, it will have destroyed me by that destructive habit and lastly, it will result to me to commit a suicide.

I have no personal solution to this, and nothing I can think of any person, who can help me from that addictive behavior, until such time, I heard from a man, the very statement of God that, "For Yahweh *(YHWH)* so loved the world, that He gave his Only Son *(King Eshua or Jesus)* that whosoever believes in Him (to King Eshua) will never be died but will have eternal life." (Paraphrased, see Book John 3:16 NIV).

A Voice in the night

Unexpectedly, in the evening of the month of August in the year of 2010 exactly two o'clock in the morning (I was ordinarily nocturnal person which means active in the night), I was personally physically, subjectively, experienced, a phenomenon above-natural, as far as I've remember was, I was silently crying in my bed, felt uncomfortably, hopelessly, guilt-overpower-me. Suddenly, an audible man's voice echoed inside my room. The voice was saying to me, *"Come now, let us reason together, though your sins is like a scarlet, I shall make you as white as snow."* As what my memory recalls it.

Later in life, I found that voice inside the book called, Book of Isaiah; chapter one verse eighteen, it says, "Come now, and let us reason together, though your sins be as scarlet, they shall be as white as snow; though they be red like crimson, they shall be as wool." (see. Book Isaiah Chapter-I, article XVIII NIV)

All I can say in response to that very night was, "Yes", since that personal event happened, it was the start of my personal quest to search for Him, to know his mind, his purpose, his intention, his manual. In him there's deeper meaning because only in him, you can find the original meaning for your existence. In manufacturer's

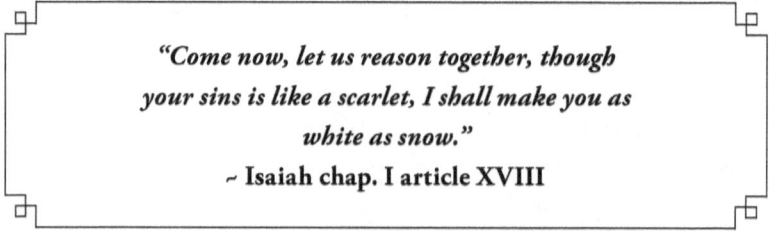

> *"Come now, let us reason together, though your sins is like a scarlet, I shall make you as white as snow."*
> ~ **Isaiah chap. I article XVIII**

analogy; His original intention established first before He invent his product. If life was valuable to him and purposely design by Him, the Divine Manufacturer; the Source of All, then, this life was design-filled with his meaning and unique value of purpose fixed to his creation.

May this book serve you, as one purpose, to help you discover your unique timeless value, and your own God-given purpose in life which will cause you to engage the world ("World" in Greek concept is *"Kosmos"* which means "system of control or systems of government or area of influence) and acknowledge Him, the True Source of our human dignity of value – Jesus the Christ of Nazareth – The King of kings and the LORD of lords, my chief-cornerstone.

Glory to King Eshua (Jesus) forever and ever, Amen!

Values or Value

Values are principle that we value and that are necessary for us to function by and fulfilled our higher purpose. Values are simply our inner convictions of what we believe – *original truth.* Truth in an idea which is valuable, it defines our attitude, actions habits, and determined our destiny. Value comes from, price equal to the intrinsic worth of a thing; standing, reputation, from Latin "valere" which means "be strong", "be-well", "be-of-value", "be-worth". Value or values are merely intangible things, even if, we don't see or touch; they are as real bit as any physical object. People may dedicate their entire lives or even surrender their lives to pursue their values, as so many loyal nationalists have done fighting for the *value of freedom, justice, human-rights, care-for-the-poor, sick, and oppressed people,* during the past-centuries from all over the nations, race, gender, time, and generations. Values can be correlated through our beliefs, principles, accomplishments, and shall be determined by its Source.

Values and Principles

The Values energize our behavior while the principles influence the result of our behavior. In Construction analogy – If values are the structure of the building, then principles must be the foundation of the building; therefore, in every value, it must be established and fixed in the inherent principles of life, created by the spirit of the King itself, King Eshua.

Values and Accomplishment

Values are convictions of our deep belief of what is most important in life. Which influence our decision and actions, which will effectively produce Accomplishments: Values come from our inner passion which fuels by your sense of vision, produced by a sense of purpose, convicted by sense of truth.

Source of Values

The Source of values is our philosophy (philosophy simply means "*philo*" means "to love" and "*sophy*" means to "think", or simply means *what we love to think and believe and embrace as true*. Philosophies produce a belief system that which results of the things we value. Values are simply what are valuables in life, it determines our morality, or morality is the product of our values. Morality informs our ethics (ethics is like a personal contract between yourself and life-principles). Morality dictates that I can't violate my values, ethics produce character and character becomes our life.

Anything that influences our actions must be started of what we value in life. There are at least two roots of values that we can be classified; one is from our human experience, civilization, and cultures, while the other is from the eternal, absolute, fixed, transcendent principles of the manufacturer itself.

Human experiences – Since the dawn of our human civilization, we are capable of learning and acquiring new human wisdom, understanding, and knowledge. Values that come from this may result from the collective human understanding based on our cultural-mindset, religion, political thoughts, and educational training system.

Second, is from above – All unique individuals that are directly / indirectly experienced and received a revelation (or vision) or Illumination of truth that which manifested inside the world system. They discovered the essence of what we call the *Truth of Self-Existent One, The Source, The Divine Manufacturer,* expresses itself as fundamental *"foundation" of all values* in the universe such as love (agape), joy, peace, gentleness, patient, kindness faithfulness, goodness, and self-control.

They recognized that the more you imitate and believed his Right values, the higher you rise in life and the more enters your inner being (heart, soul, and sprit) and expresses it in your daily-life. The wise perceived that these values are derived from original source of *"truth"* and expresses these truth values, stepping stones of our human values.

Values as spiritual

Moral values are spiritual, like a physical object that dictate our accomplishments. Our moral values tell us, if that accomplishment is right or wrong. Just as like the physical object is as real when we fall on the ground, we hurt ourselves. If some-one steal your things, "we say", "It's unfair, that's not right, or its injustice. So, as the moral values tell us why the reality if good and evil, from safe choices to bad choices, from right actions to wrong actions. It shows us from our own personal experience that if a man steals from an old woman or a mother sold his own child, or a traitor sell his own country for money, it shows us real problems, that these events are not generally accepted by any nations or societies, whether what we believe as human philosophy, such as any different kinds of religion-background. Regardless, of religious belief, we accepted this as a *"norm"*. means its normal to all kinds of belief system that whether what is the color of our human race, loving your neighbor as to the-same degree of loving yourself, or giving oneself as a sacrifice for his own family, people and country, to die as a hero of a nation for the cause of freedom, this are all examples of our moral-values because we are all moral-beings.

Part -1

The Purpose of Kingdom Values:

REASON -1

Right Values drives right behavior

"Things only have the value that we give them"

- Moliere

In my college days

Score years ago, as I started my college days in Cebu city, Southern Philippines. I take-up a course that my parents used to told me, to take BSc. In Electronics and Communication Engineering without asking anyone regarding on what this major course will be as naïve as I was, I started in the year 2001, as I engaged through the months of the semester, I found myself to be in the last position, hardly understood the lesson.

I've never understood and applied what the Instructor thought us to do. So, in order to passed my entire academic subjects, I did what can I do, and all that I did was to cheat, copy my classmate's assignments, projects, and written exams. I did not value anything with regards to my studies and also my parent's responsibilities in sending their financial supports to my studies, and I was living in a false image, deceiving myself, acting as if, I was serious in my studies.

The truth was, I was living below my potential and also, in addition, below of what my parent's expectations. As the semester ended, I've got the school final test and results; I passed it, but I know personally, I was supposed to be failed in many of my subjects. School year passed, we had an experienced crisis in the family. My parents decided that they will again transfer me from Cebu City, to our home Island, Samar, Philippines.

Before I was transferred to Cebu, I also studied in Manila, one year before I lived in Cebu. They did their best to support my studies in college but because of the higher education expenses soon, I returned again to where I was started, back in my home city, Calbayog, Samar, Philippines. Now my dreamed to be graduated in a prominent engineering school in Manila or Cebu was gone and now, I am backed to the place where I was started. I dream that, If I can graduate from any famous engineering schools either in Manila or Cebu that was promising for me, any outstanding names of State Universities in the Philippines, all of this dream was gone and now, I am back again to the place where it starts, to accept the realities of life.

As I thought before that any prominent universities will help me and my family to land in a good job and to increase my self-concept of value, that entire dream was lost. All of my parent's savings are gone, as I thought, I was afraid that my parents will eventually learn the truth about me, my lack of character that I wasn't able studying academically in school and had a bad-habit of procrastination and laziness when it comes to schoolwork.

As fear in my mind grows, I started to repent (repent in Greek word means "to change one's mind or change the way I was conditioning my thoughts, to train again to think back again to the original), open my notebook and my books to recap all I had learned.

For almost two months while it was summer, day and night for the next sixty-days period before the next enrollment comes, I re-studied again all of my academic subjects in our home for fear to failed the assumption of my parent's expectation and bring shame to our family's name.

As an elder brother to all my siblings, my brother and sister thought or should I say had a high-regard towards my studies. In other-words, they are proud of their eldest brother, as they thought I was real, but, in reality, I was not. For fear that, I don't want them also to be discouraged because of me; I reviewed all over again, changing the way I think about my studies.

After that summer passed and self-studies finished, motivated by fear, revealing my true lack of character and to my family's expectation, I realized one thing; I saw my parent's valuing my studies because they don't want me to experience the realities of high-rise unemployment job inside the country.

My mother was one of a casual employee in the city council government of Calbayog (*"Sangguniang Pang-lungsod ng Calbayog"*). Both of them sacrificed their time and money for my own future. In order that, I may land in to a good company, have a job-security, therefore, help my siblings and my family alleviate the scarcity and poverty of life.

Then school year open, now the enrollment was completed, classes started. In the first test examination of my very first academic subject, I got the result that astonished me; I had a complete perfect scored. Finally, all of my subjects with regard to the major of my course, I've got almost all, near to perfection or some are perfect. Even the departmental screening exams – I received the first high-remark score in all engineering department and discipline.

For to me, previously in Cebu, cheating, lack of character, poor-study habit and suddenly, now, in my hometown Calbayog, nearly I completed mostly my entire subject near to perfection. My personal confident became stronger and stronger as the days goes by, from a lazy, procrastinator student into an avid reader – I've seen a different and complete turn-around behavior since my repentance (repentance means - changing my attitude or changing the way I condition my thoughts in my mind).

3

I discover in myself that the capacity of learning is not based on any type of schools whether it's private or public, also, it's not based on the quality of teachers/instructors, and not also, based on any kind of situations or circumstances of our lives, but it was all inside of me. I was 100% responsible for my own life, and not just on my studies. As well written by one of the first century writer/philosopher in his epistle to an ancient people, he says,

"Therefore, it is because of Him who is able to do surpassingly, more than we ask or think, according to His ability (potential) that is working

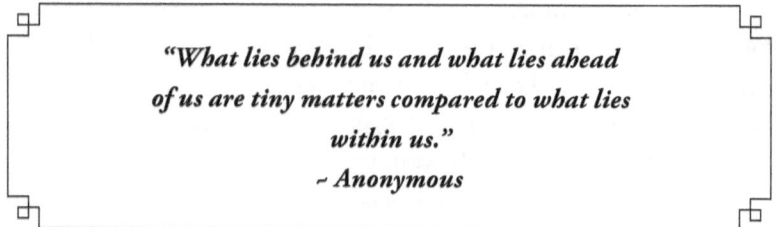

"What lies behind us and what lies ahead of us are tiny matters compared to what lies within us."
~ Anonymous

within us." (Emphasis added by parenthesis, see. Book of Ephesians; chapter III, article XX1, for you to review the complete statements).

The Principle of Seed

What it means above was, the ability of a "thing" is within the "thing" itself. As one of the famous anonymous author quotation said, *"What lies behind us and what lies ahead of us are tiny matters compared to what lies within us."*

Our value gives us meaning in life, it gives focus and sense of urgency and it provides us a roadmap, plans, strategy, and re-priority in life. Values are important items in life that are treasured within our personal belief, that eventually will have produced influence and impact individual persons, families, society, and the world itself, whether in a positive or negative sense.

Values needs source

The Purpose of Values gives us guidance in our daily decisions – "The Light". Living a life that portrays positive values will correctly present the light of our values. Everything in the universe has its own source, including values. Here in this book, it's starts with the idea of the Divine Creator, his express idea.

As an ancient proverb says, *"To respect the LORD* (LORD in Hebrew concept means Mighty Owner or Master) *is the foundation of all knowledge, but fools* (fools in this statement means morally-bad) *scorn wisdom and training."* (Emphasis added by parenthesis, see. Book of proverbs, chapter-I, article VII).

A young Jewish master-teacher living in a time of Roman Empire, in the reign of Tiberius Caesar, His name is King Eshua (Jesus), said this:

"You are the Light (Light which means "knowledge of the truth of God's law and principles) *of the world* (world means "kosmos" it refers to the area of influence such as, but not limited to; banking, education, politics, media, sports, business, religion, etc.) *A city established on a hill which can't be unnoticed."* ("City on a hill" is an idiomatic expression which means *visible*). (Emphasis added in parenthesis, see. Book of Matthew, chapter V, article XIV).

Right Values needs foundation

Right values must be founded somewhere, it must have a foundation. Every building constructed must be first established by a sense of foundation – built and design. Here in this book; every value is founded on the following principles of the "Kingdom of God" established by the "King" itself. The LORD Eshua (Meshika or Messiah).

Right Values and Lighthouse

As previously stated above, I mention about the Light Which King Eshua (Jesus) mentioned. One of great signs and guidance along the seashore is the Lighthouse. Whether in storms, hurricane, and typhoon-monsoon, or in a bright-morning quite calm day, lighthouse will always stand. That's why in the ancient days until now, most of maritime vessels look for guide along the seashore.

As we go along in this book; may I propose to you some of guidelines that we can learn through the lesson made by the lighthouse.

Principle of Lighthouse

Right values must be founded on the following principles of the "Kingdom of God", which sometimes the synonymous of Kingdom of God can be "Kingdom of light", so let's study the *lighthouse* that carries the light, thus, as to Right values that carries our behavior – Right values drives right behavior.

1. Right Values – First, it must be stand on a firm foundation. Like a lighthouse, every structure must be fixed on solid foundation. Every value with solid foundation will never be shaken, as an ancient proverb says, *"The wise build his house on a solid rock while the fools (fool means morally-bad) build his house on the sand."*
   Notice, both builders experience same storm, crisis, and problems. Crisis will reveal your foundation - Whether your values are on-place above the rock or sand.

2. Right Values – Acts as a magnetic compass. Like lighthouse it gives sense of direction. Right values are those values that acknowledge people human dignity and also, the Source. These values provide guide pointing to the true north. Every journey in lives maybe up and down, right or left, but there's always being a standard or an absolute reference

from whence our behavior and action must be based. It sets to dictate our behavior.

It is an intangible commodity with a sense of worth and great asset to our life. Values in this present age are currently changing due to socio-political and cultural clashes of all nations due to globalization. Our values should never be anchor to the principles of this world system. It must be stable, even if, people, society, culture, morality, and nations might change due to preferences and relativism (relativism simply means a kind of philosophy where it says, there no truth, and no meaning, therefore, it leads to Cynicism (*pessimistic point-of-view*) in life.

Right Values is a transcendent point of perspective where your values are not affected by the system of influence of this world but by based on the principles or "keys" of the "Kingdom of God" (better country) of the Creator.

3. Right Values – serves as security monitor. Like lighthouse it serves as to monitor the ships being colliding to other ships or gives warning ships being closer to the seashore. Right values serve as clue whether our behavior and actions, are to collide with other people or are we colliding with our own selves' personal ethics. It gives us a sense of warning and option to decide – a choice to make or break, or to fight or to flight, our values does not stop us, but it will give us an alarm to think twice from the cost of our behavior.

4. Right Values – are silent. Like lighthouse, it is obviously silent. It never has a loud speaker or a mega-phone outside the structure, it is just visible. Same as with our right values, it is silently true: quite in a sense of being right. If you follow the right values, it will eventually give you peace and joy in your heart, that these values produce right destination. Right values are as silent as a lighthouse, there are silently right. They are silently true, but if you don't listen, it will affect you whether you choose it or not. Consequences are the entail of our chosen values.

5. Right Values – are like statue. Like lighthouse it is fixed, it never moves, even if the storm is coming, it will never compromise itself; it will stand up-right in the midst of storms. Lighthouse is always right, you can't break a statue of lighthouse that sets on a rock, when you collide yourself with it, you are the one who will be break – It is always right and stable. So also, Right values can never be threatened by any person, community, society or a nation, why, even if all people or countries does not approve its values because they have their owned personal preference, Right values will always still in effect and will affect our generation and the next generation. Right values are all-the-time stable, fixed, and constant through-out all generations.

6. Right values – offers safeguard. Like lighthouse it gives a sense of peace, when you follow the lighthouse, it will give us sense of protection from being lost in the vastness of sea. Right values also give us a sense of peace within our self. It gives us protection from the vastness of "sea of life". Right values give right destination; it gives warning and shelter from the harmful effect of life. It will protect us from all the unnecessary consequence. The key of values is it drives the costs of our behavior. Right values adhere to the timeless principles or keys of life which our Source (Creator) itself built-in. If you take the short-cuts in life, you'll pay the prize for the loss of confidence and trust. Therefore, let's build our personal life and adhere to the eternal values of the "Kingdom of God" principles (which will later discourse in Part-II of the book, entitle: "The Priority of the Kingdom Values").

REASON -2

Right Values gives
right destination

"Your beliefs become your thoughts, your thoughts become your words, your words become your actions, your actions become your habit, your habit becomes your values, and your values become your destiny."

- Mahatma Gandhi

Value of Freedom – Nelson Mandela

One of the greatest leaders of the 21st century, most famous from the South Africa, received a Noble peace prize, admired leader, is the name Nelson Mandela. He is the one who is renowned for "valuing" human equality in his own country, the freedom for all ethnic-race and gender, and a sense of peace for everyone. He was simply born in the land of Africa and as the years goes by, he was living in the farm together with the animals in the forest and jungle of Africa.

He was full of energy playing as a kid in the farm-land, until such time, he deeply realized that he's freedom was only available inside the jungle of Africa and not on his own people inhabited his country. So, he got by this Idea of Freedom for all human and later in his adult-life, as his deep conviction is formed and fixed. He became a freedom fighter inside the courtroom of South Africa for his own people and lately, paid the prize of being a prisoner for due

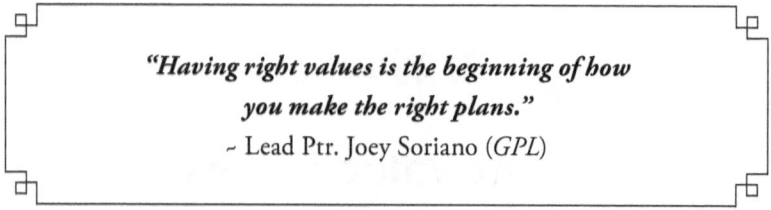

"Having right values is the beginning of how you make the right plans."
~ Lead Ptr. Joey Soriano (*GPL*)

to his opposition to the government of South Africa for almost nearly three decades of his life, still he's character and his moral values was fixed and so deeply rooted to the right values of timeless principles of the Creator, that every man and woman (as God's own product) is created to be equal in the sight of our Manufacturer/Source.

He dismantled the rulers of his country and became suddenly the president of the South Africa in the year of 1994. From this point, he became the most beautiful model, that – greater values lead you to your greatest destination. he exemplifies that value of character are the most potent armor we can have; he shows us the way to greatness is to serve the people according to your unique God-given-gifts. He is "man of value" from prison to president; his character is statue, a remarkable example of humility, giving-up his personal ambition (best-well-paid attorney) versus his personal vision for his own people of South Africa (value of freedom).

Now, what I've observed and learned from this one of greatest man lived on earth was that, "A right values gives us right destination in life".

Right destination

Right values are simply a set of beliefs that are highly important to us and serve us as our guidelines to our personal decision and action in life. Right values merely protect us from abusing our own God-given-purpose in life; which answer the question, "why I am here on earth?" and leads us to our life's destination, "where am I going after this life?"

Right values give right destination i.e. a person who values integrity will have a higher probability of success in any job, career-path, family, business, politics, media and social-community rather than a deprive person who values – drinking alcohol, gambling, stealing, cheating, womanizing, selling illegal drugs, lack of integrity, and compromiser of his personal "contract" values (i.e. selling his deep conviction for a poor porridge) will be destined to his/her own personal destruction.

Right plans and destination

Having the right values makes us aware of our life-destination. Our values will eventually produce a sense of personal vision "or destination" that will later produce a roadmap (*or written-plans*) in our lives. As my parent in the faith of said;

"Having right values is the beginning of how you make the right plans." Quote from; Ptr. Joey Soriano.

Right destination will dictate your plans in life, i.e. (in this airplane-analogy) - if the airplane destination will be Riyadh, KSA. First things first, before any airplane takes-off the runway. The pilot "must" ("must" means it is required) submit a destination and flight-plan to the Air-Tower authority before it leaves the ground. After all the necessary fuel-food-people management, the airplane will now take-off the runway. The pilot will begin to execute and stir the plane automatically according to the flight-plan (*similar to our written-plans in life*) itself. And, from time to time, the pilot must communicate to the Air-Tower to listen to, why, because only the Air-Tower can see all the airplanes in the air and it has the only capability to monitor and locate every position of airplanes at each moment. The Tower will guide you along the flight-plan the pilot makes, The-same with us, after we personally discovered our purpose (vision) in life, we must surrender it to Him our King (The Author-of-life), and begin the journey of our belief to execute our plans according to our life-destination and flight-plan. And also, from time to time we must listen to the voice (*or word*) of our King (Air-Tower) for guiding us along this life-journey. As an ancient proverb says;

> *"Trust all in the Almighty Source, in your entire course, always acknowledge Him and He will guide your ways."* (Paraphrased - see. Book of Proverbs, chapter III, article V-VI, for complete review).

Chapter One in a Nutshell

The Purpose of Kingdom values

A. Right values drives right behavior:
1. Values and value are keys and principles that we value – necessary for us to function by and fulfilled our higher-purpose to benefit others more than ourselves.
2. Values energize our behavior while keys and principles influence the result of our behavior.
3. Values always come from your Source: Truth – it comes from your Image and which image comes from your Source.
4. Right values must be fixed on the cornerstone of firm foundation.
5. Right values act as a magnetic compass.
6. Right values act as a security monitor of our life.
7. Right values are silently true.
8. Right values are statue, fixed, and also our foundation of our moral-character.

9. Right values determined our protection, defense, and precaution in life.

B. Right values gives right destination:

1. Right values must be rooted inside the foundation of objectively, absolute, moral-values of the Source/ Manufacturer.

2. Values dictate the way to your destiny.

3. Values comes from your habit, your habit comes from your repetitive actions, your repetitive actions come from your words, your words, comes from your thoughts, the pattern of your thoughts, comes from your belief, and your belief comes from your deep convictions, and your personal convictions *"must"* come the Source which is the *"Truth"*. Truth is the original, unchanging, absolute, in reference to a person, which in this book deals about the "Kingdom "and which, acknowledge the King's will, original intention, desire, moral, and his royal values.

4. Having right values is the beginning of how you make the right plans.

Part -2

The Priority of Kingdom Values:

Priority defined as, "state of being earlier." from Old French *"priorite"*, from Medieval Latin *"Propritatem"* which means "facts or condition of being prior". As precedence in right or rank; Priority means *"first thing first"*, to the right to proceed others in order, rank, privilege, etc.; Highest or higher in importance of values which given special attention with and for a purpose.

Managing priorities is our number one responsibilities; why? Not everything in life can be done. Everything has its own season and Time; Therefore, our existence has a definite lifespan. In other words, *"Prioritize the right values"*.

We should first think the right thoughts from the very words of our King, meditate, and study it. Everything has to be started in an Idea, even the unique message of our Author King Eshua (Jesus) has started with "God's big Idea" *(see the Book of John, chapter I, excerpt: "In the beginning was the word…" – The "word" here in Greek New Testament translated as "LOGOS" which means God express Idea or Gods expression of an Idea or God's big Idea).* His Idea was more important not only for me but also for all the humanity sake, the message about the *"Kingdom of God"*.

The "Kingdom of Heaven values" corrects our priority or re-prioritize our lives. As one of the ancient writer's points;

"As final point my brothers and sisters, whatsoever things that are true, pure, honest, just, lovely and of good-report; if there's be any right value, and if there be any worthy of admiration in it (things), ponder on those things." (Emphasis added by parenthesis, to review the complete writings, see the Book of Philippians, chapter IV, article VIII).

REASON -3

Right Values corrects priorities and organize

"The value of life is not in the length of days, but in the use, we make of them; a man may live long yet very little."

- Michel de Montaigne

God's big Idea

Right values come from right-thinking the right keys/ principles, or truth in life *(In the ancient days, truth they called it "precepts")*, an attitude of a mind and heart. By the way the "heart" in the ancient concept means "inner or below mind" which means "sub-mind" or what we called in psychology today as "sub-conscious mind" where as compared to the "mind", "mind" means in this book is the "conscious mind" where all ideas are received.

17

Thinking an Idea and accepting it as self-evident truth (that process of accepting the precepts or original idea is what we called "concept"), produce a belief (conceptualization takes place) and will eventually become your conviction, thus, The Idea will possess you.

That conviction will now determine your attitude (*attitude* means how your mind thinks or how you see yourself or how do you see the world in your eyes) and your attitude will drive/influence your behavior and dictate your values.

One of my greatest mentors (in my personal view), whose moral values about teaching life-principles was totally different and turning up-side down all kinds and famous theory of our popular psychology as of today, This person who lives in a small Palestinian colonized by the Roman Empire in the fifteenth-year of Tiberius Caesar was the name "Eshua" (in Syriac Aramaic/Hebrew) or in Greek/Latin/ English derivative means "Jesus" was a master-teacher (master-teacher called in that days as "rabboni" or "rabbi" which means as of today as experts, or Ph.D.). He was the master-teacher of fisherman and farmer, and turns them as world-influencer. His teaching and his ultimate "big-Idea" or shall we say, big-picture of his message was the message about "The Kingdom of God" or synonymously "The Kingdom of Heaven", or in some first-century writer such as "Saul of Tarsus" who became as "Paul" in the New Testament, he mentioned this as "The Kingdom of Son" or "The kingdom of Light".

The Kingdom of Heaven – as a country, an "invisible" one yet, it has an effect (results) and affects (influence) not only our personal values but the entire human values of the world.

Kingdom

Let's define first the Kingdom what it means. Kingdom is a place or land where the ruler of the land was called a King. His place is located from a distant place called "parent-country". He rules that land by his personal will, desire, moral, and personal values. Reflecting all these values to his citizens was his main influence to his land. Kingdom glory is in the land, they expand (Unlike, democratic concept – democratic does not colonized or expand territories) and that's why the King extend his dominion on a foreign land and make it as a "colony" of the parent-country.

"Colony" means a foreign land ruled by a Governor sent by the King from his inner-court as a "Representative" of his authority and over-all government in that land which is the colony. Kingdom therefore, is ruled by a King or Queen, located from a parent-country and aims to colonize (expand) to other place for the expansion of King's territory (called domain), exercising his dominion *(means ruler-ship/kingship)*.

The King's motivation is to influence the land esp. the colony by his personal will, purpose, his original intention, and desire for his people (called citizens), to its domain. In order that, his purpose will live a mark, imprint, an inspiration, and an impact of his personal glory *(by the way "glory" in Hebrew concept means "true full-weight of his nature" from the word "kabod")* to the colony by his life-style, culture, moral-standards, and his unique personal values.

Lordship

Inside the Kingdom, the King "automatically" owns the land by legal-rights by means of his birth. Lordship means "Legally-owned" or in Hebrew, it means "Adon" which means "Almighty Owner". In Greek/Latin they called it "Kurios" which means "Master-owner" or their word as "Caesar".

Keys of the Kingdom

Keys in the ancient time symbolize as "access". Until this time, in the year 21st century Anno Domini, the word "key" refer to us "to lock/to unlock a door". Original "keys" originally came from the Owner *(sometimes the thief has its own key but it is fake, the purpose is just to steal, kill, and destroy)*. When you bought your car, the Manufacturer will automatically give you the key of car. Keys will always come from the legal-owner of the manufactured things itself.

Also, Keys in the Old Testament book (in Torah in Judaism culture) refers as "Authority"; see the Book of Isaiah XXII article XXII

Apparently, "The King of Kings and LORD of lord" gave his keys to his disciples (disciple in Greek concept 3101 "mathétés" which means leaner or student), so, the students of King Eshua (Jesus) received apparently the keys of the Kingdom of God (for complete review; please check the Book of Matthew/Mark/Luke/John (or in Eastern culture Syriac-Aramaic called "the Peshitta") in the book of Matthew, chapter XVI, article XIX, The King said to them,

"I will give you the keys of the kingdom of heaven; whatever you bind on earth will be bound in heaven, and whatever you loose on earth will be loosed in heaven." (See the Book of Matthew chapter XVI, article XIX, NIV).

"Bind" means "to lock" and same as opposite to "loosed" which means "to unlock", the King meant that, he gave his students the authority coming from Him as King to access from His Country Heaven, that whatever you agreeing with another person here on earth *(colony)*, it shall be done among you.

Keys are also called principles or sometimes called "truth" or in the Book of Psalms *("Zabur" in Islam)*, written by a King name David, he called the keys as "precepts" *(which means: A general rule intended to regulate behavior or thought or precepts simply means "before instructions or before warning).*

There are many keys *(original principles or truths)* found and written by his students of King Eshua, but I have only taken the nine "keys" of the country of Heaven built-in by the King in his creation which will be effectively, if it will be used properly, to impact and influence the world by his personal royal values to his royal colony.

(Note: The "keys" where I found these were located in the Book of Matthew, chapter V, article I to XII of King's constitution, but more often they called these as "beatitudes" but for me, these are original keys of the Kingdom of God where, if and only if, you used these nine basic keys in your life, I know for sure that the King's word will never be broken. Anyway, in the Kingdom – the King's word is a law, the King's decree says "heaven and earth will pass-away but His words will never").

9 "keys" of the Kingdom of God

These are many keys mentioned in the book of Matthew, Mark, Luke, and John (the 4 good-news about the Kingdom of God and with our LORD Eshua "Jesus"), one thing before we proceed with 9 keys – we must remember that "keys" are to be used in times of opening and closing a door (if you don't mind – this is only a reminder!), even if, I the author of this book, will not use these keys of the Kingdom of God, even I can't experience the benefits of the "keys" of his country message. Also, even if you knew these 9 keys after reading this book, and if you improperly or misuse the "keys"; In-short you don't know which "keys" for specific door to unlock or lock (you know that by your own experience – we can't experiment in using keys to a door which one will work-out for us), it will never also work-out. So, these keys need to be familiarize with you by heart, like the keys in your own house and car (you don't experiment the key in your own car, you know which *exactly* key you will used for your car, from your own experience). So, experimenting with the "keys" doesn't give us advantage over those who haven't the "keys".

Here's the nine "keys" of the Kingdom of God:

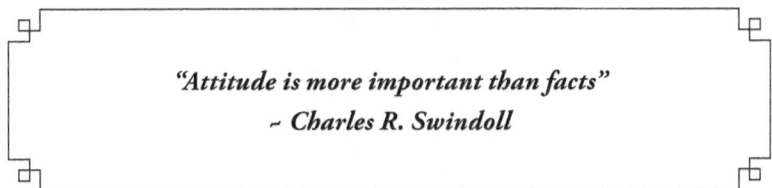

"Attitude is more important than facts"
~ Charles R. Swindoll

1ˢᵗ key is "Attitude"

Attitude – you're wondering why? What is attitude? Before I precede this subject about attitude, this is one of the most important matters and most widely written by people over many centuries – whether He or she is a political-leader, professor of psychology, behavioral scientist, teacher, artist, famous sport-figures, religious-devout people, or even a mother with five children's down your neighborhood, everyone has an attitude. Whether rich or poor, famous or unknown, they have some-kind of attitude.

According to the two sources of dictionaries – In Cambridge dictionary, it says that, a feeling or opinion about something or someone, or a "*way*" of *behaving*:

And the other – In oxford dictionary, it says that, A settled "*way*" of "*thinking or feeling*" about something. Origin from late 17th century (denoting the placing or posture of a figure in art): from French, from Italian "attitudine" 'fitness, posture', from Late Latin "aptitude", from "aptus" means 'fit'

Many books have written on these topics and many authors' deals with this subject. From a practical motivational point-of-view, to the complex-theory of human psychologist, they have their own definitions. As the French philosopher once said, "*I think therefore I am*". "Thinking" begins in our mind, and our mind is powerful.

From one of the inspirational man – author and educator, that I used his quotation every day and believe in his quote, even if, before I was formerly atheistic-naturalistic-worldview. I believe in his statement that,

> "*Attitude is more important than facts*"
> ~ *Charles R. Swindoll*

It was taken from his literary works: His complete quotation of that was, "Attitude is more important than facts. It is more important than the past, than education, money, circumstances, than failures and success, than what other people think, say, or do. It is more important than appearance, ability, or skill. It will make or break a business, a home, a friendship, an organization. The remarkable thing is I have a choice every day of what my *attitude* will be. I cannot change my past. I cannot change the actions of others. I cannot change the inevitable. The only thing I can change is my attitude.

Life is ten percent what happens to me and ninety percent how I react to it." – I rest my case.

Attitude define to me, is our *"mental-disposition"* simply how our mind thinks. It is the mental state of a human-being. It is our thinking-skills of what we love to think, or our philosophies in life.

According to the King recorded in the book of Matthew, He said,

> *"Blessed are the poor in **spirit**, for theirs is the kingdom of heaven."* (See book of Matthew, chapter V, article III, NKJV).

Notice the word "spirit", not capital "S" like the "Spirit". When you look the meaning of spirit in the Greek New Testament, the word (spirit) means *"pneúma"* (G4151), The Hebrew counterpart (rûach) has the same range of meaning as G4151 (pneúma), i.e. it likewise can refer to *spirit, wind, or breath.* According to Strong's Exhaustive Concordance; the word (spirit) is figuratively, a spirit, i.e. (human) the rational soul, (by implication) vital principle, *mental disposition.*

Small letter "s" in the word "spirit" means spirit-of-man, or our inner-man, or our inner mental disposition, while the big letter "S" means the spirit of God, or spirit of truth or The Holy Spirit.

That is why, when you read the book of Joshua specifically in the chapter of XIV, article XXIV, The LORD GOD YHWH spoke:

> *"But My servant Caleb, because he has a different spirit in him and has followed Me fully, I will bring into the land where he went, and his descendants shall inherit it."* (Review the book of Joshua chapter of XIV, article XXIV, NKJV)

Please again notice the word "spirit" in that passage: it refers to their human-spirit or attitude, the *"way of their thinking"*, remember that, Moses ask twelve spies to check the land. Each of the twelve men look the-same land, people, fruits, animals, etc., but Only the two of them "interpret" what they see and gave a good report rather than the ten spies who gave negative report based on their attitude or the way they *"interpret"* what they've saw.

The attitude of the *citizens* of the (country) Kingdom of Heaven – has a clear distinction from all the kingdoms of the earth due to their different values system. Kingdom values are simply influence of the culture of heaven by the values of the King itself and it is resulted to the way and how the colony thinks.

If the world values will have resulted to fear, the Kingdom values resulted to produce "faith" (or trust) in the King. If the world is worry about many things, kingdom values do not worry because all-of-these-things (In the context of the book: "things" mention there refers to what we eat, drink, and clothes) shall be added into us. If the world values say, everyone is doing that, like stealing, murmuring, complaining, mind-yourself-first, don't look for others concern, be proud of your achievements, be successful even though in the process you hurt everybody including your family and yourself, as long as you reach your goal and be successful, all these kinds of values from the world gives different attitude system, while the King values system says,

> *"The King will reply, 'Truly I tell you, whatever you did for one of the least of these brothers and sisters of mine, you did for me.'"* (See the book of Matthew XXV, article XL, NIV)

Therefore, the King says; if you consider others more important than yourselves, then you will be rewarded. Each of us should look not only to our own benefits, but greater also, more than the welfares of others.

Kingdom values begin with our minds – "Kingdom mind-set" Attitude that's precede by distinctive unique kingdom values which produce a distinctive culture right here on earth. Kingdom of Heaven culture is on earth. The Priority of King Eshua reflects in his personal prayer which he taught his students recorded in the book of Matthew chapter VI or Luke chapter XI (see the complete chapter). He said,

"In this manner, therefore, pray: Our Father (Source) in heaven (parent-country), Hallowed be your name. Your kingdom come, your will be done on earth (colony) as it is in heaven. Give us this day our daily bread. And forgive us our debts, as we forgive our debtors. And do not lead us into temptation, but deliver us from the evil one. For yours is the kingdom and the power and the glory forever. Amen."

When the New Kingdom takes-over the colony, the old culture values of the colony vanished; it will be extinct and therefore, replaced by means of influence of the new government "Kingdom of heaven" "attitudes" which later produce a kingdom culture on earth – this is the primary concept of colonization.

2nd key is "Compassion"

We live in the twentieth century in the world of individualism. In democratic country especially, individualism is top priority goal of everyone that leads to self-government. The main issue today, in most part of the world due to democratic principles of capitalism, many people right now are either falls on the two group; namely the "haves" or "have-not". The gaps between the two groups become more and more set-apart. Few philanthropists are existed today such as the business icon Bill Gates and other else are devoted their-selves to the poor, alleviating, and helping them, especially of many third world developing nations.

Compassion - from "com" which means "with or together"+ "pati" "to suffer" (see passion). Simply means "to suffer together" with people, this trait is one of the Kingdom values of the country of Heaven. The best example of this is our King of Kings "King Eshua", who from the very beginning of time was the "Word-of-God or Logos (Greek) or Miltha (Syriac-Aramaic)" which means the express idea of God the Father (Abba in Hebrew) in the form of flesh, sent by Abba, to the colony, to save that which is lost. As was recorded in the book of John., *"For God so loved the world ("kosmos" which means the system and also the inhabited of the system), that He gave his only Son (King Eshua), whosoever believes in him (King Eshua) will never perish, but have an eternal life."* (See the Book John chapter III, article-XVI).

That is the main example of compassion, exemplify by our gracious King. He said, which is recorded in the book of Matthew V, article-IV, says;

> *"Blessed are those who mourn, for they shall be comforted."* (See book of Matthew, chapter V, article IV, NKJV).

In this season, we therefore cultivate our relationship towards our families. Showing compassion is the sign of confidence coming from love "agape" (which means God's love). Compassion is showing genuine concern and care for the needs of others. One of compassion traits is encouragement, in which, one is uplifting people and cultivate the spirit of cooperation, alleviates the suffering, oppressed, depressed, and suppressed society in the world. As once said by Mother Teresa to his monsignor, *"If I can't feed a hundred people, then I start feeding just one"*, she says also, *"begin the nearest of you"*.

True citizens of the kingdom of God: starts for the cause of helping people, even if, they are alone in a mission.

The King compassion gives us promise and decree it by his authority and it was recorded in the book of Matthew XXV says that;

> *"Then the King will say to those on His right hand, 'Come, you blessed of My Father, inherit the <u>kingdom</u> prepared for you from the foundation of the world: for I was hungry and you gave Me food; I was thirsty and you gave Me drink; I was a stranger and you took Me in; I was naked and you clothed Me; I was sick and you visited Me; I was in prison and you came to Me.'* (see the book of Matthew chapter XXV, article-XXXIV to XXXVI, NKJV).

He is the greatest model of compassion – In which the King himself values the people and together with-their suffering in this world, He paid the price for our liberation and true freedom to dominate again, as it was written in the beginning.

"To dominate the resources of the earth, fish, birds, animals and all the livestock's, and all the earth's creatures, but not including men." (See the Book of Genesis chapter I, article-XXVI to XXVIII).

3rd key is "Self-discipline"

In these days, most of cultures lived in a careless, wasted, meaninglessness lives. From the food, they ate at many fast-foods, to the block-buster movies they've attended, from watching sit-com in their living room, playing cards, gambling, membership of elite-social clubs, fraternities, sororities, using social-medias, and other online internet excessively to the point where he or she is departed from his/her world, not mentioning the people who've addicted-substances such as but not limited to i.e. *heroine, shabu, ecstasy,* and many forms. The modern man today is assaulted of many life-distractions which are in-time paralyze the victim and leave the poor man or woman or even a child slave to his own deadly-habit, negative passion, destructive appetite, and cynic-attitude.

Religion tries to answer this dilemma, Yet, in my own opinion it doesn't solved the problems of the humanity. Sometimes, if not all, religion encourages you to be divided amongst your brothers and makes you wait for another life's miracle coming from heaven, eliminating the principles of management. Time is one of the wisest counselors have ever given to man. If time is gold, then time is the most precious commodity of every human-living (man and woman) thing in the face of the earth.

Sadly, many people ignored the *"management of time"* itself and many other forms of his resources such as but not limited to i.e. money, God-given-gifts, family-relationship, and etc. One of the wisest man ever lived was the named, King Solomon. In which he's sayings recorded in the book of Proverbs (*wise sayings*), it says that in the chapter XXIX, article-XVIII;

> *"Where there is no vision, the people perish: but he that keepeth the law, happy is he."* (See the Book of Proverbs chapter XXIX, article XVIII, KJV).

> *"Where there is no revelation, the people cast off restraint; but happy is he who keeps the law."* (See the Book of Proverbs chapter XXIX, article XVIII, NKJV).

Notice in both translations of the same article, the word *"vision"* is interchangeable with *"revelation"*. Vision or revelation doesn't come personally. It is not personal generated idea. It is an Idea from Source *(A divine one)*, what I mean is, this idea came from The Source not from my own mind. Every vision came from a visionary which is in this book came from the Mind-of-the-Source *(The Anointed King Eshua)*.

In that article, basically vision determines your destiny. Vision is the source of our personal, national, and corporate discipline. Without vision *(purpose in picture)* people throw-off their self-discipline, self-control and lived a life of being loosed, unsound-mind, abusive to his/her own life. Vision is so important, that it is the source of our hope in the future (unseen). Vision is not a function of the eyes but a function of the heart. It is the driving-force which grasps the future "unseen" into manifesting it into the "seen" world.

Every scientific invention, business-industries, medicine, political and social changes happen in the past centuries was because of a *vision* of man or woman. From Mahatma Gandhi vision – Freedom of India, to wright brother's vision – airplane, to Bill Gates business empire – Microsoft, to Steve Jobs – Apple, to Martin Luther King, J.r. (vision: "I have a dream" speech) – Social Equality Rights, and many more. All of these major changes in the society were because of one vision (aspiration combined with passion); yet believe first by one man, the carrier of his/her vision, which comes from the Source.

Therefore, As the King says;

"Blessed are the <u>meek</u>: for they shall <u>inherit</u> the earth."
(See the Book Matthew. chapter V, article-V, KJV).

Meekness does not mean weakness; it refers to exercising God's strength under His control – i.e. demonstrating power without undue harshness." The word "meekness" comes from the Greek word *"prautes"*, which depicts the attitude or demeanor of a person who is forbearing, patient, and slow to respond in anger; one who remains in control of himself in the face of insults or injuries. In the Greek language, the word *prautes* ("meekness") conveys the idea of a high and noble ideal to be aspired to in one's life. Although an injurious situation may normally produce a rash or angry outburst, a meek person is controlled by kindness, gentleness, mildness, or even friendliness.

As Mr. Rick Renner says;

> *The word "meekness" pictures a strong-willed person who has learned to submit his will to a higher authority. He isn't weak; he is controlled. He may in fact possess a strong will and a powerful character; he may be a person who has his own opinion. But this person has learned the secret of submitting to those who are over him. Thus, he is one who knows how to bring his will under control. In rare instances, the word "prautes" ("meekness") was used to describe wild animals that had become tame because it correctly conveyed the idea of a wild, fierce will under control.*

Thus, meekness is "strength under his control" as like as the "train-lion" will inherit the earth, promise by the King itself *(earth can refer to a land or real-estate)* due to his/her self-discipline, self-control, and gentleness-strength.

29

4th key is "Right-desire"

There are few good desires of a human - Starting from his or her family, career, community, society, and nation. All of our desires or human-will comes from our inner-man. It comes from our heart. Right-desire is a strong desire which comes from "being-right" with the "Authority" *("Authority" in this book refers to the King's will in his country and government of the Kingdom)*.

The King decree:

> *"Blessed are they which do hunger and thirst for righteousness; for they shall be filled."* (See Book Matthew. chapter V, article-VI, KJV)

"Hunger" and "thirst" are one of the most beautiful mental-pictures which can be mean as "need" and "desire". When you are hungry and thirsty, you are seeking for something – food and water. The King decree that, if you truly seek his country and you *"Align"* (the word *align* refers to "being-right" with the head or authority of the government or country) yourself to the Authority *(King's will)*, that means righteousness. Righteousness is not a religious word. It came from a legal root-word "rights" which can be access only by the "law-abiding-citizens" of that country.

Beautiful example of righteousness is like; my wife Susan came and lived inside the Kingdom of Saudi Arabia together with my two little children's. As they lived inside the country, the government of KSA decrees that for every overseas worker living a family status inside the country there must have acquired an *"Iqama"* (*"Iqama"* means a national I.D. system of the country) including his/her family as his/her dependent. For every dependent, there's a tax required by the gov't. Paying the government legally and with submitting correct necessary documents according to the King's decree, we are eligible, bonafide, legal-entity, expatriates living in Kingdom of Saudi Arabia.

Therefore, if you are truly need and desire to live "being-right" to the authority, whether it is your parent's, police, priest, or people with authority to your life, you will be satisfied. "Filled" simply mean satisfied; it produces contentment. A godly contentment which only the Source (King) can only supply and no other.

> As an old hymn says: *"Delight yourself in the Almighty-Owner, and He (King) will give you the right-desires of your heart."* (Emphasis added. See book Psalms chapter XXXVII, article-IV for complete review).

Desire is simply means a deep-passion more than death, birth by a sense of purpose *(original design or Owner's intention)*, by your original assignment. Inherently, Right-desires give you a sense of personal-value, significance, high-esteem, and self-worth.

5th key is "Forgiveness"

In our society, we've seen a great devastation of people, coming from many broken-families, economic-depression, and high-crime-rate. Today's society believe that, if you are being attacked, insulted, injured, whether-by actions or words, our two-seconds initial-response to the offender is the-same – to retaliate.

One of many observations, in life is that, forgiveness is more powerful than hate. Forgiveness is more about decision to forgive a person, even if your emotions aren't there, *"forgiveness is costly"*.

Why it is so hard to forgive? First, our natural-inclination is to revenge and to forgive also is to accept the offense of the other. "Forgiveness" is costly because we agree to live with the *consequences* of another's mistakes, rather than taking it out on him/her. However, we will live with those consequences one way or the other. Our only choice (free-will) is whether it will be in the bondage of bitterness or the freedom of forgiveness. Your enemies become temporary because forgiveness makes them win again as your friend.

Forgiveness is the pill that cures us from all the bitterness, chronic-disease, cancer, and ultimately death. Forgiveness is the key to self-freedom which produce internal peace and security in our lives. It is the most valuable key that the King decree.

The King says, *"Blessed are the merciful; for they shall obtain mercy."* (See Book Matthew. chapter V, article-VII, KJV)

6th key is "Character"

This is one of the most common problems among all nations, from the global perspective, to the smallest basic-unit of our society, our family. From the ancient agricultural times to our modern 21st century information-age; every leader from the president, prime-minister, business corporate managers, investors, bankers, politicians, scientist, teachers, priest, pastors, imam's, any religious groups, including parents such as our father and mother, everyone are looking for a character.

Character is so subtle; it is one of the most important key in our modern life. Most people are failing on this test. Why, that this it is most important than reputation? How can I have a firm-character? What should I do? Is there any training or teaching to people to improve their character?

First let's differentiate what is reputation and character. Reputation is what people might see in you *(or think of you)*, while character is who you are when nobody sees you. Character is the manifestation of our personal values in life. It is the container of our gift, it is the effective tool on earth, more important than our gifts and talents, more than important than words.

Character established our inner life. It protects our personal purpose, vision, and safeguard our potential. It protects us from cancelling our personal vision or aborting our life's purpose permanently.

Character is to live legacy from your unborn children and children's children. Right values must come from Kingdom principles, why? Principles are necessary for function. In the building construction analogy: if the character is like the tower-building, the principles must be the foundation of the building.

The greatest enemy of character is *"compromise"*, in-short; your personal values are for sale. Character is only developed through time, from test and trials. Character begins with our philosophy *("philosophy simply means "to be in-love with your thoughts that you believed in it.).*

Our belief creates values, values produce morality, our morality produce personal ethics *(ethics means your personal contract between yourself and the life's principles)* and your personal ethics is your behavior and actions which determines the outcome of our character.

Right character is always the same yesterday, today, and forever – it never changes. That's why our alphabetical and numerical numbers are called characters because it never changes. Number 2 will always be number 2, even if, you are on the moon, underneath the earth, or even to the farthest corner of the universe, it will never change. Even if, what time in a day or night you use, numbers and alphabets will never be change. That's why, it is called character.

Statues are also character, like previously example, the statue of liberty in the United States of America and our famous Filipino Dr. Jose Rizal monument are called character, why? Even if, the storms, hurricanes, monsoon-rain, or sun-light, or any weather, they will never be change. That's why, it is called character.

> The King decrees again, He says, *"Blessed are the pure in heart; for they will see God."* (See Book Matthew. chapter V, article-VIII, KJV)

Characters are not make in times of crisis, crisis will reveal it, whether we have it or we lack of it. Character can be tested in three ways: first test is the appetite (such as i.e. pleasure for food, water, and sex), second test; is for power, and third test; is for human-pride. All of these test and trials will reveal our character. All of that test will never be gone in our human-lives, it will constantly monitor, and shows what our character will be.

7th key is "Peace"

The globalization makes every nation inter-dependent to each other. Due to mismanagement of earth resources from extremely greedy businessmen, our natural resources like petroleum-oil are being fighting for by each sides of some ten percent of elite-men in the world trying to control the overall ninety percent wealth of the earth. It is sad that the only last thing commodity we have, is to have secure and peaceful lives. Peace is one of the most valuable promises by any leader, in every election happening in the world, Yet, it is the most difficult to achieve. It is like chasing the wind.

All of countries and nations and kingdoms of this world can't and will not ever produce self-generated peace. From the dawn of our civilization to our modern technological advance society, peace will always be temporary.

But don't lose hope, why? In this world, we will have many troubles, as the King of Kings and the Lord of Lords is reminding as which is written in the book of John (see John chapter XVI, for your review).

I Notice that, in the ancient book of Isaiah (see Isaiah chapter IX, article VI-VII, NKJV) the promise says;

> "For unto us a Child is born, unto us a Son is given; And the <u>government</u> will be upon His shoulder and His name will be called Wonderful, Counselor, Mighty God, Everlasting Father, <u>Prince of Peace</u>. Of the increase of His government and <u>peace</u> There will be no end, Upon the throne of David and over His kingdom, to order it and establish it with judgment and justice from that time forward, even forever. The zeal of the Lord of hosts will perform this."

See the underline word, our King's government has and will always be in peace that no has no ends. It's wonderful to hear from this ancient book that his Kingdom (country) are naturally, and self-generated, peaceful. Because our King is the also the Source of Peace and He is called Prince of Peace *(prince means ruler – he rules in peace)*.

> He reminds his citizens again, in his royal decree;
> He said, *"Blessed are the peacemakers; for they shall be called the children of God."* (See Book Matthew. chapter V, article-IX, KJV)

Peacemakers are initiators of peace; they are active and not passive in promoting peace. Peacemakers are inherently peaceable within themselves. They are the resource of peace and they understand that most of people are in battling circumstances, life-crisis, and therefore, instead of fighting with each other, they tend to help other's need.

Peace is like a fruit, the fruit of the tree depends on the nutrients, soil, and sun-light but the tree doesn't produce by any nutrients, soil, or sun-light. The fruit (peace) is produce by connecting to the vine (Vine represent the symbol for our King Eshua or Jesus) itself. Without the vine; the soil, nutrients, and sun-light will have no effect on the fruits.

Therefore, peace is not trying to be living peaceable to all people, whether with or without others, you have peace that comes from the vine (or other words from the Source). Peace depends on its Source.

A person who sows peace will always reap a harvest of justice. Peace comes from the Source and Sustained by Him. People who value peace make his/her life focused, and make other influence.

Recently history shows that people who valued "peace" makes difference in his/her life generations. i.e. Mahatma Gandhi, Martin Luther King, Jr., Mother Teresa, Nelson Mandela, and our Filipino Dr. Jose P. Rizal, all of them are influential kind of leaders who personally impact society with their core values more than violence. The peace in the "Kingdom of God" is one of the core-values of the King and his beloved royal-citizens.

8th key is "Righteousness"

Continuously, one of the keys of His Kingdom is - His Righteousness. Righteousness is NOT a religious word, activity, rituals, or tradition (trade-*ition are trade to the next generations or transferred*), it has come from the root-word "Rights".

In context of countries, such as citizens *(legal-entity of a countries and countries have no members)* has the "rights" and "privileges" given by the law of country, produced by the constitutions. Righteousness is a legal word, that pertains to "properly, judicial approved (the verdict of approval); it means justified by "believing it in Judge's approval, which It refers also to what is deemed *("deem" means ownership-rights)*, rights by the Lord after His examination. (Lord in Hebrew concept means Almighty-Owner). The King judgements is giving rights and justice for his own people (His Kingdom citizens).

> As an old epistle to the people of Hebrews says, *"But unto the Son He (Abba) said, thy throne, O God, is for ever and ever: a scepter of righteousness is the scepter of thy kingdom."* (See book of Hebrew chapter I, article VIII. KJV and reference also to book of Psalm chapter XLV, article VI, KJV).

By the way, scepter can't be found in any democratic concepts and ideas. It can't be found on any presidents or even a Prime Minister type, why, because the "scepter" can only be found in the type of monarchy which is the Kingdom.

Scepter is the sign of The Authority of the King, and He always hold it with his right-hand.

> *"And in Your majesty ride prosperously because of truth, humility, and <u>righteousness; and <u>Your right hand</u> shall teach You awesome things."* (See book Psalms chapter XLV, article IV, NKJV).

The other symbol also hold by the King is the Sensor which symbolize by his Royal-influence, and lastly with his crown which simply means His Power to dominion over his territory-land and his colony.

Only in His scepter of the King points to you means, He declared you are righteous in his eyes, in which written by his student John in chapter I article XII, NKJV, the beloved, brother of James, son of Zebedee), says;

> *"But as many as received Him, to them <u>He gave the</u>*
> *<u>right</u> to become children of God, to those who believe*
> *in His name:"*

Watch-out for the word "right", because he gave us by means of pointing His scepter into you, and declared that you are by His "rights" are one of His Sons and daughter of His Royal family, in believing in His Name.

One of the most important reminders by King in his student's writings was in Matthew - written in chapter VI, article XXXIII, which says,

> *"But <u>seek first</u> the <u>kingdom of God</u> and His <u>righteousness</u>,*
> *and all these things shall be added to you."*

There are ONLY two focuses of our King Eshua (Jesus) in our lives. Many of our motivational speakers always talks-about this so-called the "Law of Priority" which covers all aspect of our lives. One of each law of priority famously quoted from the Italian economist is named Vilfredo Federico Damaso Pareto, which named after him the "Pareto principles – the 80/20 rule" which states that, for many events, roughly 80% of the effects come from 20% of the causes, or from Mr. Robert Kiyosaki quotations with regards to financial literacy – he called the "90/10 principles", which means that, "all of the 90% of wealth of a countries were controlled by an elite of 10% people and vice-versa.

37

Whatever the percentage you observe – 90/10, 80/20, or 70/30, you see that general principles of Priority are required for us to be effective in whatever our goals, roadmaps, and vision in life. Let's go back to the Kingdom keys of Priority which state by the King (the underline word), that if you "seek" *(seek means diligently pursuing, studying, motivated searching)*, next; "first" *(first means priority, notice what the divine manufacturers made – he made only two things to seek and no other)*, first also simplified our lives from many complicated things of these life.

All of I observed from few successful entrepreneur top-business people around the world, they have one in common, they're so focus on "One thing" they dominate, and that they always say, *"One thing I do"* this phrase you always heard from them. What it means that, they found their purpose and vision and they focus all of their energy and time with it.

For me one of the greatest mentors I have is the King. Notice even his famous greatest commandments, He summarizes it into two – he makes it simple. Therefore, in life we need only to be focus in two things (according to this book); Kingdom and Righteousness. Everything will be added unto you. If you focus and/or prioritize your life in two things; i.e. God and family or whatever two things you need, just like a magnifying glass that focus the beam of the sun in one focal point – the result is efficient, intensified, powerful and very effective. Righteousness is the right-alignment to the Authority (government/country) by-laws and constitution.

9th key is "Purpose"

> ""*Blessed are you when they revile and persecute you, and say all kinds of evil against you falsely for My sake. Rejoice and be exceedingly glad, for great is your reward in heaven, for so they persecuted the prophets who were before you.*" (See Book Matthew. chapter V, article-XI, NKJV)

The Power of Purpose is one of the most important keys of the Kingdom of God. Once the purpose is established, it will take over your life and possess you. You become "authentic" by being true to yourself, because you are so unique "in-charge" or "authorized" in

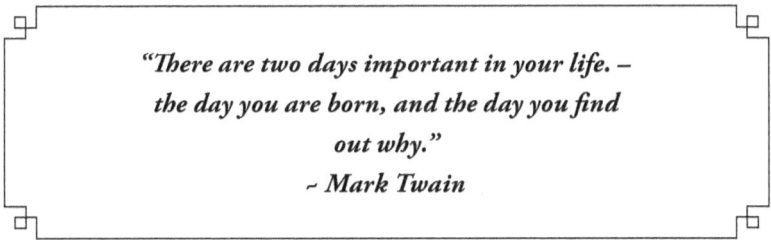

> *"There are two days important in your life. – the day you are born, and the day you find out why."*
> *~ Mark Twain*

one specific assignment given by the Author. Purpose is the key to significance; self-meaning is generated by-itself. People who've recognize their selves know their self-value concept and has a deep passion for doing and Fulfilling their assignment to the world *(world in Greek concept is "kosmos" which means "systems of government" or "area of influence").*

Helping and building people lives for the common good of humanity us their primary vision in life. The values of purpose are birthed from knowing "why" I am here rather than busy in doing many things in life. As Mark Twain says, *"There are two days important in your life. – the day you are born, and the day you find out why."*

God's purpose (King's purpose) is greater than any problems, greater than poison, greater than any pain. His purpose shall always prevail. Mission or purpose is not only important individually but also same as true for corporate business world, political system, banking, educational, society, and total government. It is more vital to know "why" than in existing and doing everything without knowing what meaning of our presence here.

In reality, if you notice the manufacturer, every manufacturer's creation serves its purpose, from the tiniest plankton organism to the gigantic supernova of balk-hole inside the visible universe, everything has its own purpose and function. Even if, all created things are beautiful, the degree of beauty or aesthetics doesn't eliminate the purpose of "why" the thing exists in the first place.

REASON -4

Right Values inspires dedication

"Virtue is a state of war, and to live in it, we have always to combat with ourselves"

- Joan-Jacques Rousseau

Father's advise

Both of my parents offered their lives to train us, for us to be well-mannered respectful well-being person. They value of it so much, that most of our family expenses goes that time to our learning. Until economic crisis - hit us again, in our family in the year 2016. After I went to Manila for taking-up Board examination, I went home in Angeles city, Pampanga. It was the house of one of close-relative's (mother-side), they have two homes', so we are just temporarily occupying the other house of her, if not for my aunt's generosity, we will not be in this phase of my life. Through her my aunt, we lived in Pampanga for a reason of my exam's preparation together with my family, in order we can start again our lives back, and find job-opportunity.

We lived in the second unfinished house; with no Main door access, only a curtain, opened all the time, and with no light-fixtures inside the room except a small study-lamp, and a comfort-room with no-roof. Most of the times, if rain or storms came by in Angeles city, before I take-a-bath, I was already wet due to the weather-condition. But still, we are thankful to them and deeply appreciated them, for their open-heart and generosity.

As my aunt's family, help us find to breakthrough and to thrive in the middle of recession, I remember that clearly, my mother chose temporarily to be employed as nanny (babysitter) near-by. My mother became a house -maid and babysitter in order to survive us for our meal in one day. That time, I have no job and still focusing only in my studies.

My Father was a labor in construction and has paycheck casually, and also, I have two more siblings still college and high-school student. Every night when my family goes to sleep, I spent time studying for my up-coming licensure examination, even-up to a time where all of my cousins and their friends had small parties frequently, they always invited me together with them, to drink, eat, sing-a-long, but because of a higher-purpose, I had to choose not to participate in any parties.

I personally value what my Father told me many years ago, He said,

> *"Son, don't you envy your friends right now, even if, it seems they are living cheerfully in any happenings, parties, etc., it is just temporary. My son, keep what you are doing and later you will reap a harvest on what you sow."*

Principle of Delay Gratification

This above statement suddenly, I realized that in life; a "principle of delay gratification" – we must be somehow willing to pay the prize for our dreams. Dedicate my life for and with the purpose of fulfilling and helping the family, and in order to achieve my personal goal "to pass the national-licensure-examination". To get a job, help my parent, also help my siblings, and fulfilled my responsibility as an elder brother. I was passionately doing all-of-that for a cause

Three years later, I received a phone-call from an agency, little I know; this was the beginning of my personal journey inside the Kingdom of Saudi Arabia. For eight consecutive years, I only spent one company, finally my entire sibling now is graduated from their studies, and they've their own job as well.

This book also I dedicate to my family: My Father Mr. Jesse Z. Casiguran, who was in my former years, serves my guide and my mentor. Also, my Mother Mrs. Maribel F. Casiguran, she was my inspiration and resource of my hope and also, my two siblings; Mr. Jesse F. Casiguran, my close-friend and buddy, and Ms. Michelle Marie, our blessed little sister. For without them, I can't reach and achieved our family goals, so my appreciation goes to them.

Living example of Abraham Lincoln

The Principle of delay gratification works for everyone. It works in every-season, and every country, as long as you are willing to pay the value (worth) of your dreams. Similar to a man who fails many times in his personal-career, even his marriage life, whose name was written in the United States of History. He was the 16th President of USA; His name was Mr. Abraham "Abe" Lincoln.

For me and as far as many historians are concern – Mr. Abraham Lincoln was one of the most unsuccessful men in many terms of his political-social and personal married life. But, one thing I know from his Biography *(written by Dale Carnegie – Lincoln the Unknown),* He was consistent and persistent at his core-values about fighting for the cause of human-dignity against human-slavery, whether in legal-court, in politics, or even in his own town, he was simply acknowledging the eternal value of a human-being from the eyes of Divine Manufacturer.

Since, He values this principle more than his family; He became amazingly nominated unpredictably to the office of presidency of United States of America. Without no idea, how he became nominated, and all of sudden, He became the 16th President of USA in the year of 1861, without hesitation in his deep-conviction, He issued the famous "Emancipation Proclamation" that declared forever free those slaves within the confederacy in 1863.

He was one of the most beautiful models illustrating that - values inspire us for lifetime dedication to be, cause. Abraham was more dedicated to his core-values "human-equality", just like also the name of Mr. Martin Luther King Jr., He personally value the civil-rights of all people, and became more dedicated to his set of core-values that even if, He was threaten to be assassinated, he was still more dedicated to the life-principles, more than his own life. That's why Right-values inspire perpetual dedication.

Right values give us self-disciplined and determination to reach our right destination. Destination is destiny – dedicate is simply means "giving of oneself to a purpose or higher-cause". Your daily dedication reflects what's you've value. Dedication begins when you discover your purpose, even if, you lost your life. You decide to commit to meet the cause for the sake of reason rather human self-preservation, no matter what's the cost. Dedication is weigh given over exclusively to a single use, or assignment or purpose. It comes from a deep belief and convictions fulfilling that reason. Dedication in Latin means "to devote, consecrate. Dedication I purposely surrendering to a higher-cause and motivated by passion and deep sense of significance of why we are existed.

Chapter Two in a Nutshell

The Priority of Kingdom values

A. Right values correct priority and organize:
1. The Kingdom of Heaven values corrects our priority or re-prioritize our lives.

2. Right values come from right-thinking the right keys/ principles, or truth in life, an attitude of a mind and heart.

3. Kingdom is a place or land where the ruler of the land was called a King. His place is located from a distant place called "parent-country". He rules that land by his personal will, desire, moral, and personal values.

4. Inside the Kingdom, the King "automatically" owns the land by legal-rights by means of his birth. Lordship means "Legally-owned" or in Hebrew, it means *"Adon"* which means "Almighty Owner". In Greek/Latin they called it *"Kurios"* which means "Master-owner" or their word as "Caesar".

5. Keys are referred to as mean of "access" or symbolizes as "authority. Keys in the Kingdom of Heaven mean that, there are many keys (principles) that can be used to lock or unlock the country of Heaven by simply using these basic keys or principle of the country to influence the colony earth.

6. Right values come from the King's personal values.

7. Right values are influenced by the Kingdom of Heaven principles which are as follows;

    i. Attitude (King's mind)
    ii. Compassion (King's desire)
    iii. Self-discipline (King's character)
    iv. Right-desire (Right-alignment with his desire)
    v. Forgiveness (King's mercy)
    vi. Character (King's values)
    vii. Peace (King's nature)
    viii. Righteousness (King's Judgment)
    ix. and Purpose (King's original-intention and his greatest commission to his citizen).

8. Attitude or *"mental-disposition"* simply how our mind thinks. It is the mental state of a human-being. It is our thinking-skills of what we love to think, or our philosophies in life.

9. Compassion means "to suffer together" with people.

10. Self-discipline is meekness and it means "strength under his control" as like as the "train-lion", due to his/her self-discipline, self-control, and gentleness-strength.

11. Right-desire is a deep-passion more than death, birth by a sense of purpose *(original design or Owner's intention)*, by your original assignment. Inherently, Right-desires give you a sense of personal-value, significance, high-esteem, and self-worth.

12. Forgiveness is costly because we agree to live with the *consequences* of another's mistakes, rather than taking it out on him/her. Forgiveness is the pill that cures us from all the bitterness, chronic-disease, cancer, and ultimately death. Forgiveness is the key to self-freedom which produce internal peace and security in our lives.

13. Character is the manifestation of our personal values in life. It is the container of our gift, more important than our gifts and talents, more than important than our words. Reputation is what people might see in you *(or think of you)*, while character is who you are when nobody sees you. Character are statues it never changes, it is forever stable. Character established our inner life. It protects our personal purpose, vision, and safeguard our potential. It protects us from cancelling our personal vision or aborting our life's purpose permanently. Character can be tested through appetite, power, and pride. Test and trials will never be gone in our human-lives, it will constantly monitor, and shows what our character will be.

14. Peace comes from the Source and Sustained by it. People who value peace make his/her life focused, and make other influence.

15. Righteousness is the right-alignment to the Authority (government/country) by-laws and constitution.

16. Purpose is the original intention or design by the manufacturer before producing. It is the cause or reason "why" it is existed.

B. Right values gives right destination:
1. Right values breathe self-discipline and self-determination to reach a destination.
2. Right values are giving-up oneself for a higher cause or purpose greater than our two personal motivations: self-preservation and human security – no matter, what is the cost.
3. Right values are aligned to the king's cause and purpose.
4. Delay gratification is subjecting us from temporary pain for the greater costs and benefits of our future-destiny (vision).
5. Values dictates the way to your destiny.
6. Your daily dedication reflects what you value.

Part -3

The Power of Kingdom Values:

REASON -5

Right Values interprets vision

"Although gold dust is precious, when it gets in your eyes – it will obstruct your vision."

- His-Tsang Chih Tsang

My Wife's dream

My wife, Mrs. Susan Puyo Casiguran, was arrived in KSA, the year 2015 of the month of February 27th. This was her personal dream to go outside of our home country Philippines. One of her greatest and most rewarding opportunities she can experience, prior of her arrival was, she started to dream this at the age of twelve, and she believed that nothing is impossible as long as she believes; it is always her motto in life.

She is the eldest of all her siblings. As early as it seems to be, she became the key-helper of the whole family and the "bread-winner". She worked hard, she believed that even if, she didn't accomplish her college degree, and she believes that she can reach any goals, she want in life.

She values her belief that she can reach success even without college diploma through business selling and networking marketing. She always keeps treasured what God promised to her. She values her dreams to the point; she believed that goals in life will be met accordingly in King's appointed time, as what she always declaring promises to her family. She envisions her vision that her destiny in life will be determined accordingly to what she valued and not on what she saw and experience temporarily.

Finally, after six-years waiting patiently, in the year of 2014, after endeavoring of processing, her permanent visa, and her plans became reality, and her dreams of going outside the Philippines became true, that almost every one of her friends was besides her, accompanying her going to Manila International Airport. It was a day of vindication, what she valued, and her attitude makes her dream possible. As an old famous writing says, "With man this is impossible, but with God, all things are possible."

Right values determines your destiny

"Right values determines your destiny", where Am I to go? The question of destiny

Ideas come from a mind. Idea is invisible but powerful, it is indestructible, it can have outlived people, surpass time and season, travelled throughout many generations, from one civilization to

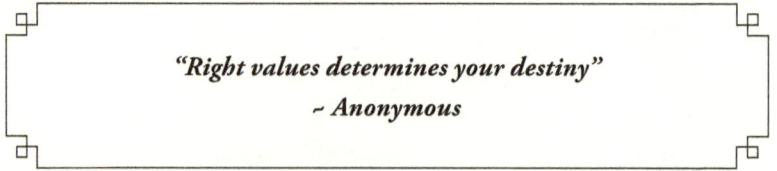

"Right values determines your destiny"
~ Anonymous

another. Ideas can live forever. Our lives are based on our ideas, ideas that you believed. What you are now in life are all based on those ideas what you value and believed.

What you believe, you valued

What we believe – we value (a matter of attitude).

Right value comes from an idea that your belief within you, that encircled your life. Idea is thought, a big-picture that gives meaning. Vision is the capacity to see the future that traps in you. It comes from an Idea that generates the meaning and creates your passion, later will absorb everything.

What you understand is what you respond

What you understand is what you respond – perspective.

Vision is critical to every person's life; people are perishing because of lack of vision (destiny). Vision is not sight – sight is based on current situation present not on future. Vision starts from an idea and you believe it and assured by it.

Vision originate from the *Source* itself, that your belief, it is true and you start to manifest it by simply focusing on that vision that Creator gives you. We can look at one picture but yet we have many interpretations according to the belief we have, it's perspective or worldview; it's how we view of the world we living in.

Value in life will determine the outcome of your destiny. Ideas produces philosophies, philosophy builds your belief, beliefs determines your values, what you value dictates your life and your destination.

Worth of product

The more the worth of a product is, the more the value it attracts to it and therefore, the more worth the vision of the manufacturer is.

You are paid by what worth you have, people will pay more to something or someone, if they see it is worthy. Worthy is the measure of items express in value. It is amount we exchange to the value. The higher the value you have, the higher the worth it is, the higher it deserves and praise.

Every manufacturer places their image in their product and the vision of every manufacturer is that their image will be protected entirely so that they regard value to their own product before it reaches to the consumer.

Manufacturer will guarantee its product for their name sake because of the image they emboss to the product is guaranteed to be success according to the standards and testing of its product. Therefore, the worth of a product depends on the integrity of the Manufacturer to protect the Creator vision and purpose.

You give worth - what you value.

Vision is the source of our determination. It fuels our passion. It gives self-discipline and it determines our destiny.

REASON -6

Right Values support acceptance

> "Know thyself"
>
> \- Plato

Who Am I?

Knowing my personal identity was an unbelievable, extra-ordinary journey for me. It begins with a question in my mind, "Who Am I?" (Sounds like movie), maybe one of the five most difficult questions I've ever asked in myself. As I begin in my early childhood, I look for my identity to my biological parent which is my Father, which was the source of my inspiration and strength. As I grow in my statue, I learned that, it is normal for us to look for someone who give us the courage, inspiration, and to become successful person.

In pursuing of my undergraduate studies, I thought that education and degree will give me ample successful and meaningful, significant life, as many others have said, "education is the key to success". Most people think that success is measured in our job-position, career, and educational adulation, but surprisingly, what I felt was empty and unfulfilled.

I felt meaningless and insignificant. The more personal success I achieved outside, as other's defined, the more I became dull to myself, it's like a rat-race in the mace, where everything became routine. I went to job, work for ten-hours, go back to accommodation repeatedly for score of months until suddenly, I begun to talk to myself, reflecting back on my personal life as I traveled from the other side of the globe and reach the heart of KSA. I began now my searching for the Truth. The Truth if there's an Ultimate-being, who He is? And Who Am I also? What's my purpose?

My personal journey was the same story with this parable:

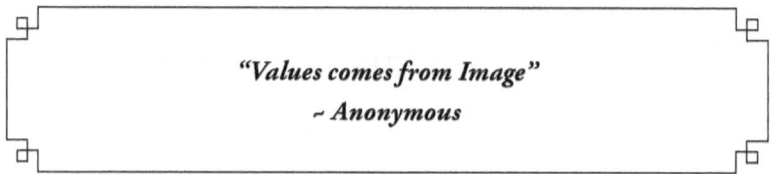

"Values comes from Image"
~ Anonymous

> "There was a man that went to look for hidden treasure in a far land, as he looked and dig for treasures, he discovers a secret treasure. The only thing he had done was, he temporarily buried this, and went back to his town, and sold everything he had before and bought again this new land, where he lays his secret treasure".

A man who found the most valuable treasure in the world; that treasured was the "kingdom of Heaven" – where he found his self-image.

In His Image

My Image can only be found from the Source, the Right-Source. The "Source" as I refer in this book is the One – True Author,

Creator, Sustainer, Self-Existent one, the Alpha-and-Omega, the Unchangeable, Absolute law-giver, and Eternal life. My personal values comes from Him, our Abba Father *(Abba in Aramaic terms means "beloved")*. Values comes from an Image. The word "Image" in the ancient literature means, "Characteristics" or "character" in-short or "nature". If my Father who are in the Kingdom of Heaven has the same character or nature that I have, and the Father is the

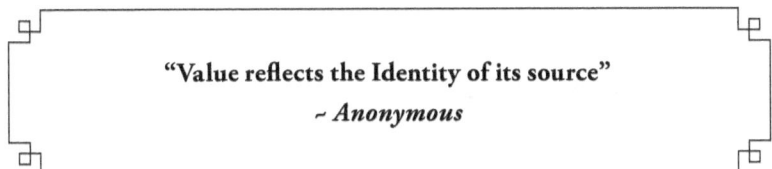

"Value reflects the Identity of its source"
~ Anonymous

source of Image, image is produce an intrinsic value, which produces worth, and so that, my personal worth (or esteem) is not based on this world, but rather from our Father who is unseen and invisible.

Manufacturer's image

Every manufacturer in the entire world places their image on their own product. From every manufacturer's product – the Identity of its products reflects the standard and specification of manufacturer. In each manufacturer, each places a value on its own product because it guarantees that its own product is successful, thus every manufacturer reputation will be determined by the success of its own design product. Whatever the value of the product, it reflects to its own manufacturer's identity and reputation.

Let's see the analogy in the creation of the earth. Fish lives in water; water is more valuable to the fish itself. The seed lives beneath the soil; soil is more valuable to the seed itself. The birds live in the air;

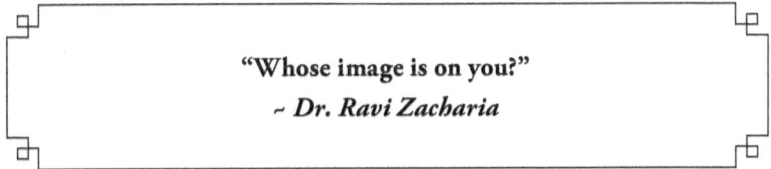

"Whose image is on you?"
~ Dr. Ravi Zacharia

the air is more valuable to the birds, so in every creation or product in manufacturing terminology has its own built-in identity which defined by the Creator/Manufacturing design values.

The Identity of the product reflects the manufacturer's values. Identity comes from the Image of the manufacturer, whatever the value of the manufacturer; it places on the product itself. The more secured the Identity of manufacturer, the higher the value of the product and vice-versa.

Value reveals the Identity of itself

Value reflects the Identity of its source. If we accept the value of a product, we know the source of its Identity, therefore, to know one's value, is to know your Identity, to know your Identity, is to know your Image, to know your Image, is to know your Ultimate Source. Be careful of what you accept and value, Value reveals the Identity of itself.

One of ancient thinker and master-teacher of life has something to say about Identity and related to its value. His philosophy turns upside-down what other might say about value and Identity, in his narrative story;

> Then the Pharisees went and plotted how they might entangle Him in His talk. And they sent to Him their disciples with the Herodians, saying, "Teacher, we know that You are true, and teach the way of God in truth; nor do You care about anyone, for You do not regard the person of men. Tell us, therefore, what do You think? Is it lawful to pay taxes to Caesar, or not?" But Jesus perceived their wickedness, and said, "Why do you test Me, you hypocrites? Show Me the tax money." So, they brought Him a denarius. And He said to them, "Whose image and inscription is this?" They said to Him, "Caesar's." And He said to them, "Render therefore to Caesar the things that are Caesar's, and to

God the things that are God's." When they had heard these words, they marveled, and left Him and went their way. (See book Matthew chapter XXII, article XV-XXII, NKJV).

If only the people ask a follow-up question what would it be, if they are genuinely seeking the truth. I think this would be the follow-up question.

"Whose image is on you?" ~ Dr. Ravi Zacharia

This question is a profound that you can think or imagine. If I ask you, who's image is on you? What would your answer would be? The Idea of Image, identity, and value are converging on this one simple question.

Identity comes from Image. Image in Semitic concept means "nature" or "characteristic" which then have an intrinsic value and are valuable according to its source.

What Image you accept, as clearly important to you – you value.

REASON -7

Right Values enables continuous Learning

"You can't teach a man anything; you can only help him to discover it in himself"

- Galileo Galilei

In my former years

As I looked back one score years ago, I and my brother desired that someday we could have discovered something beyond the night sky. We love at an early age looking at the universe. We regularly spend our time outside at the back of our grandmother's house in Samar, Philippines. After dinner: after all the house-choirs, we hastily sit-down and watch the night outside. In front of us is the ocean, and the background was a single pine tree, with a small nipa palm house *(Bahay-Kubo)* and the sounds of many insects vibrantly noise around, while the ocean waves to and fro, and staring above the sky are the countless stars.

One day as the Philippine Atmospheric Geophysical and Astronomical Services Administration or PAG-ASA told every Filipino citizen that a comet will pass-by near to us and we will experience, what they called "meteorite shower", shower on the larger part of Samar island, Philippines. Exactly as I was remembered, I woke up as early as possible, nearly as four o'clock in the morning. I personally witness the tens and hundreds or maybe thousands of falling meteorites at the back of our house. Since that day, my interest about observing the universe and discovering new things grow inside of me. That time I want to become an astronomer, reading a lot of discovery and national geographic magazines, watching science network, and reading books about science and astronomy.

In feeding my insatiable hunger about the knowledge of the heavenly sky, I thought to myself – If I could have discovered something in the heaven that will expand our understanding like once of many astronomers left their discovery in the history book of science, some people invented things in order to help the humanity, just like my personal protagonist named Nikola Tesla, I was amazed in his contribution to the science of electrical, electronics, and communication, thus, I dreamed that someday, when I reached the age of thirties; I could somehow invent, or discovered a place in the universe, or discovered principle like of many scientist over the centuries, that will contribute to the humanities knowledge expansion and human understanding.

Little did I know when my junior high-school starts, I was initially introduced to an unimaginable dark secret world, a world where your imagination is corrupted by the images of uncovered women inside the magazine, and I never told anyone including my parent and personally kept it by-myself. Time went by I focused only on college studies, pursuing the dream to be one of board-passer in the field of electrical engineering in our school – finally, as history was written. I got the passing score in my 2006 national licensure examination held in Manila, Philippines.

All of my family and sibling were happy, but in spite of success, we experienced that moment financial and relationship crisis. I personally walked two kilometers from Redemptories Catholic church to Philippine International Convention Center (PICC) with my formal suit and black shoes, just to attend the ceremony. All of my feet burst from the heat of the road and vehicles, and as I finally reached the convention center, I found out that I can't bring inside my father and my brother to witness my oath-taking ceremony, just because I don't have extra money for entrance fee (500 pesos per person), So, just for the oath-taking sake, I went alone by myself, tired, hungry, and sad what happen at that time of my National board licensure oath-taking.

Season past; I got a secure job from a construction firm in Sta. Rosa Laguna, near in Enchanted Kingdom. I spent all of my days working there in home or in the site-office. In one unusual night, without personal doubt, I was tempted by one of my peer's friend which he brought inside the house, two ladies who was that time his convive *(what I mean is they're all drinking except for me)* that night, I commit a mistake in my heart, without a doubt with this woman, whom I didn't know. From that time on, I want to forget that night – I drive myself to be busy with all activities in the job but still I was felt empty inside.

All of sudden, after two years working in the Philippines, a job order came up for me without any clue, I was hand-picked by a manpower agency. To my surprised I asked them, "Ma'am, where did you have my resume because, as far as I can remember anything, I didn't apply for a job interview for abroad", the lady response, "From the Internet Sir", It's like a matter of one unexplained event in my life.

As I passed, all of my medical report for documentation process, I've got a positive result in my urine-test; they found out that I am positive of Urinary tract infection (UTI), suddenly, a memory went up inside of my head, and maybe it was that evening with the strange woman. All I have that moment was to repent *(repent means to change the way I think)* and asked God that I will pass this second medical test before I can go to abroad. After two weeks of medication and sober, I passed the second urine-test, and this was the beginning of my personal journey to the middle-east nation. Finally, the moment of truth arrived, I flew to the Kingdom of Saudi Arabia filled with dreams and hope, to help my siblings and inspired to earn money and invest on the education of my family.

One year and one month - after my job became a routine for me. I felt again the emptiness of my heart. I tried to discover new activities, sports, attend some of parties, went-to-job even working holidays, just to be busy with everything and still filled void, hollow success, buying things, I thought I need, having drinking illegal substance inside KSA, be merry. Outside, my family and some of my close friends thought I looked like as fulfilled-satisfied, successful individual man, but in reality, deeper inside of me was eroding. I became poorest that ever before that nobody knows, I became slave to my own addiction, I'm living a double-life. I said to myself, "If there's any hope or solution, someone a person that could help me from my porn-addiction. Unsuspectedly; One day a man came into our accommodation, was trying to share good-news according to what he believes was truth. The least person I want to share with my time is this kind of religious person *(by the way, I still personally don't like to talk about any religion practices, tradition, and or rituals)*. So, I was the last person to attend in our accommodation to his invitation to listen in his message.

After hearing his message, I heard that there was one whom I can draw near and help us in our deepest needs, without finding-fault, and without condemnation, that person came again and spent months in our villa sharing the good-news. Suddenly, in the middle of the night around, two o'clock in the morning, at the moment – I was disarranged, disorganized, confused, with suicidal thoughts, shamed, and condemned, I remember the guy that used to share and proclaimed the good-news. All of my thoughts rushing to and I begin to open my mouth and said with tears in my eyes, "If you are really true Eshua (Aramaic) or Jesus (Greek/English), please help me!", without any noise inside the room, as everyone is sleep, around two o'clock in the morning, I heard an audible sound or voice, it says,

> *"Come now, let us reason together, even if you're*
> *separated from Me are like a scarlet, I will make you,*
> *as white as snow."*

All I answer was, yes! And I closed my eyes and fall to sleep. The next morning, felt I was freed from something that I couldn't explain, I began to search and looked for his words, I tried to search in the book, and to my amazement, I was surprised that I found the very exact words I've heard that night of my encounter with Him, I finally found it in the book of Isaiah in chapter one article eighteen.

I realized that I found the most valuable treasure in the world that money couldn't buy and this was his very words – The "Truth". As an old proverb says,

> *"The fear of the Lord is the beginning of Knowledge*
> *but fools ignored and hate his instruction."*

This was the beginning of new chapter in my life. Continuous reading of his words, and his message, was a priority. For almost eight years I've spent in KSA from the time I've arrived until to this day, my personal goal in life are only two – My top 2 priorities in life is to seek first his Kingdom and second seek to be right-align in his constitution *(or in any religion it is called; righteousness).*

His words are like a bulb to my feet, and it's also a light to my path, and it brings river of water flowing from my heart filling the emptiness and hunger. I am still hunger and thirst for understanding his unique, timeless, message – "The Kingdom of Heaven".

Success or Fulfilled?

As I observed the world of many great men and women over the past centuries around the world, being successful in the area of business, career, showbiz-entertainment, music MTVs, fashion, political-arena, sports, banking industries, scholastic-education program, publishing, and any other system of influence in the society, but suddenly, all of them, their personal lives were wrecked either by addiction of substance or illicit affairs that which led them to their brokenness, poverty, and some worst are death. Therefore, True learning – comes from this principle.

The principle of Valuing the fear of the Lord – is the bed-rock of true knowledge. His message about his good-news about the Kingdom of God and its influence in my daily life encourages, empowered, and transformed me to write this book. Only in his message, is the most valuable information I have personally discovered throughout my life. Until now, I am hungry for understanding how his message can bring long-lasting impact in discovering my personal potential and ability. As I read from the Old literature says, *"He gives us the ability to produce wealth"*, wealth is in terms of value and time.

Learning his truth and applied his message give us insight that makes us wise in this generation, just like the story of two builders – one builds his house over the sand and the other over the solid-rock,

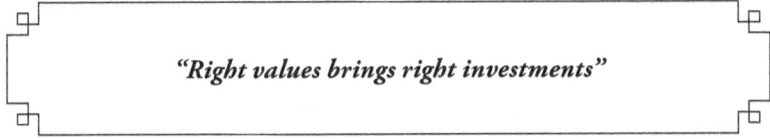

"Right values brings right investments"

storms comes and both experience same wind, the house built on the rock remains and stable, while the other is destroy. Only in storm will reveal the true nature of our values and what we've learned acquired knowledge that we've applied in our daily-life.

Right values determine your ability

Right values will determine your ability, "what can I do?" – The Question of Ability. Ability is the capacity or power to do and produce a result. Everything has an ability to produce according to its purpose and functions. Ability can be inborn, such as they called "talents" and the other one is learned through time and with a person called mentor called it "skills", both produce and affects the quality of the result.

Purpose and design affects the ability of a something, it defines the things ability.

Right values provide self-discipline, i.e. such the story of the great legend Michael Jordan. He was a normal young boy who believes in an idea that the basketball is his area of gifting and because he believes that idea of himself, he values basketball practice more than any passion sports he can do. Every night and day he practiced, practiced, and practiced in his backyard and through time and with additional mentor, right-coach, team-mate, and fans. He refined his talent, his natural ability and become skilled basketball player in his time and his generations. So, what you believe in your ideology will produce a sense of value and sense of importance to you. It will affect your discipline and it will later become your habit.

According to book of Dr. Stephen Covey, in his famous book the "Seven habits of highly effective people", there you will find that topic "Sharpen-the-saw". Where, sharpen the saw means preserving and enhancing the greatest asset you have – You. It means having a balanced program for self-renewal in the four main areas of your life – physical, social/emotional, mental, and, spiritual.

Right values bring right investments, whatever you value, you put price on it – we called it "worth" or "worthy". It means you are

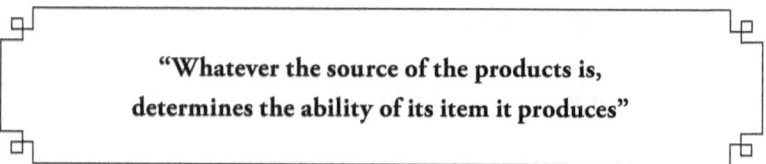

"Whatever the source of the products is, determines the ability of its item it produces"

willing to invest more time, effort, and money; in other words, you are willing to sacrifice to pay because you believe that the Idea and plans is more worth than anything or anyone in this world for the sake of your love-ones and your family.

The results of investment bring refinement on your learning which becomes your skills. That's why we spend so much time and money in our personal education because we value learning and we believe that education makes our skills more valuable and marketable, versatile, and increase our chances to be successful in terms of career we desire to endeavor.

Ability

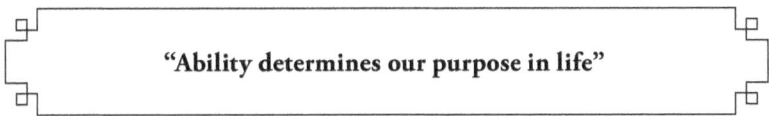

"Ability determines our purpose in life"

Ability comes from the Source or Manufacturer (when we speak about products). Every manufacturer builds a product with an ability to perform functions and results. Whatever the source of the products is, determines the ability of its item it produces.

You can't teach what you don't learn; also, we can't remind ourselves the things with what we don't learn. Learning is the basic requirements of our life. To understand the world, we are living in. Don't underestimate the value of humanity by what school/degree he or she attains. School is not equal to learning; many people believe that if you as a product of any kind of schools/universities, your ability is more likely to be success than what the person doesn't achieve, but schools can never give you talent (or in farmer analogy), schools can never give you a "seed". Schools can only refined/cultivate the seed you have, Thus, it's very important to know first what is your seed, before choosing the education necessary to cultivate and refined that seed.

Source determines the ability of the created things

One sample of analogy from creation is that, Fish comes from water, fish is made up of water itself, fish don't need to learn to swim; it's by nature that its ability is to swim by design and purpose by the Source. Fish don't attend swimming lesson in its lifetime, they are just born to swim.

Next example is the seed – The seed comes from the land, the seed is made up of earth material, seed don't need to learn to grow, and it's the seed nature to grow naturally when you plant it beneath the soil. Seed never attend tree growing-convention because they don't need to learn that ability, it's in them as seed purpose by the Source.

If you as human-being created as infinitely (spirit) and part finite by the Source, then whatever your source determines your greatest ability. Some says you came from salamander that became tadpole that became a mammal ape and that became a human through the process of evolution through million years ago, others say, you are made in the "Imago dei" (which means Image of Source/Creator/Manufacturer/God), whatever you might believe, out of that your Source will be your likeness. "Likeness" doesn't mean you have the same face with the Source, likeness means same function (In Hebrew concept).

Whatever your position maybe, whatever you believe, you value. Your Source gives you value and give its meaning to your ability, in order you to function by according to its specification or design.

Ability determines our purpose in life; whatever the Source creates, he place it inside its product itself; the ability to perform its assignment according to the mind of its Source. Whatever the Source; the product's abilities function is created by will dictate by its' purpose/design of its Source.

You are capable of anything as far as long as you believe that "we as resources are determined by our belief – Our Source which we came from".

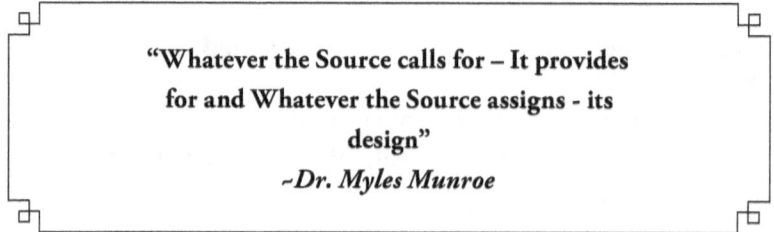

"Whatever the Source calls for – It provides
for and Whatever the Source assigns - its
design"
~*Dr. Myles Munroe*

Whatever the Source calls for – It provides for. And Whatever the Source assigns, He design. Therefore, by believing who or what is your

Source is crucial part. It's the pivotal point of our learning, the lenses of our naked eyes that which we interpret what we acquired through the journey of learning. It is the foundation of our learning, it gives is coherent and consistent worldview and it's our deep motivation that fuels our habit of continuous learning the right things.

As an old proverb says, *"The fear (out of respect-love rather than of being afraid) of the LORD (Lord Means "Almighty owner") is the beginning of knowledge and wisdom".*

REASON -8

Right Values purge old habits (To Unlearn)

"The unexamined life is not worth living"

- Socrates

"We are what we repeatedly do. Excellence, therefore, is not an act but a habit"

- Aristotle

At the grocery store

One typical, arid night, in the heart of Riyadh, Kingdom of Saudi Arabia, me and my wife Susan were outside going to buy mineral water in one of grocery store located near in our accommodation, about ten minutes ride. We finally decided to buy sixty (60) packs of bottle-mineral water where each pack contains twelve (12) bottles in it. This was a season of volume-sale discount. As I unloaded each packs of mineral water, piece by piece on the trolley, I personally sense that what I am doing aren't supposed to be accepted by the cashier in the grocery store. In my memory, my mind kicks-in and remembered previously that, if I buy more than three (3) packs of these, I will be soon rejected by the cashier because they intended not to sell a whole -sale on just one person. So, my immediate response was to comply out-of-thoughts fear of rejection, previously experienced, and what had the culture I've learned and was brought-up, that I am not supposed to go beyond status-quo, being common, and the stay-on-your-place-mentality.

It was a moment of displaying what I was mentally trained – timid, nervous, and fearful, but to my startling thought, my wife Susan emerges as she began to load all of these mineral waters going to the cashier, with her smile and pleasant-look, she boldly come

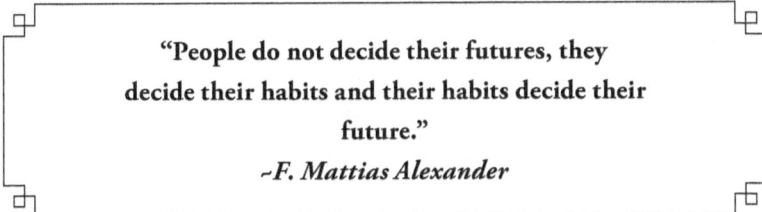

> "People do not decide their futures, they decide their habits and their habits decide their future."
> ~F. Mattias Alexander

without reluctance she faced the cashier swiftly, and there she was, with no single objection coming from any personnel of the grocery store, we passed pack by pack up to the last pack smoothly. Finally, I've realized that, we both have same opportunity, same situation, same scenario on that night, but we have differently responded according to what we have believed.

My wife is a business-type woman, early in her life she was trained to faced many rejections, Yet, she learned that for every rejection in selling (business) is just temporary experienced from the customer/people, at the end, her product always sells, thus, she doesn't give-up, it's her personal values that this is only a matter of test-of-faith, therefore, she valued believing that every rejection is just but momentarily.

It is only a secret part of the business, while me, I was conditioned to believed, culturally-trained on the status-quo of the society, being busy trying to fit-in the system.

Right values affect our habits

Right values can change our old habits such as timidity, imitation, people-pleaser, procrastinator, and mediocre. Unlearning these many old bad habits replacing by new ideas with right values concept

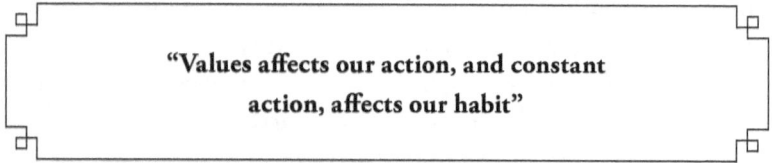

> "Values affects our action, and constant action, affects our habit"

that transcend beyond our culture, schools-education, political-structure and even religious dogma's upbringing and rest on the innate Timeless principles of life.

Right values will replace old habits by changing what we believe which will produce new results thereby, unlearning those old habits & practices created by the environment and our culture and history, through new Ideas which comes from the Source. To put simply, values affects our action, and constant actions, affects our habit. Habit according to Mr. Bob Proctor is the sum of all paradigms *(paradigm means the worldview or the personal interpretation of a person looking to the world, in which we believe it's true).*

Good habit is repeatedly good actions, first produced by our attitude that came from our philosophy and values. Right values purge old habits and continuous unlearning our previous knowledge that was based on our cultural norm. values make us stand-out rather than to be fit-in the society, difference-maker rather than being common. It is simply producing anew added value to the person. Right values guard your purpose in life. As quoted by F. Mattias

Alexander says, "People do not decide their futures, they decide their habits and their habits decide their future."

Right values determine your purpose

Right values will determine your why. Why I am here? It's a question of utility. Purpose according to its etymology; purpose comes from two words *"pur" which means "while", (French word "poser") means to put place,* therefore, Purpose is simply *"to put forth or by design,* design can be mean as plan, aim, goal, and, intention.

Purpose is one of the hardest questions any human can ask. It always asks "why", one of renaissance philosopher named Gottfried Wilhelm Leibniz famously ask, "Why is there something rather than nothing?" and the list is on and on. People in many generation ask this tough question of purpose about "why" – a question whether you are six years old boy or eighty-six years old, whether you are from the ghetto (or depressed area) or living inside a palace, whether you are black, white, yellow, red, or blue, Asian or European, it does not matter, where you come from? Everybody is asking this personal metaphysical question.

What we value in life is what we believe important in life. The more value a thing is, the more Worth the thing is, Value is simply the measure of worth of a thing; It is the price you're putting in. The culture that we are living-in are right now produce in us a mindset that values specific things in life, e.g. In these days, many people work overseas for the sake of "make-afford mentality" in life to buy something especially for families need, so to keep this cultural mindset, we tend to value our school-education high-degree because most of us believed that through school-high degree equals success. So, we can land to secured pay-job and support your families and love-ones.

I do understand that to produce cultural values it must be teach and re-in-force to the minds of the people. So, to change our life-style we must first change our personal values, to change our values, we must change our belief's. What we belief is what we value. In order to learn a new thought in life, we must change our beliefs and hence, we tend to change our values, to unlearn what our culture says vs our personal belief based on what we value. Value reflects his purpose we learned. It protects our destiny – it gives self-discipline to fulfill our original purpose in life.

Unlearning the values of this world "kosmos" or "system of influence" is a hard thing to do; we need a paradigm-shift from our old ideas into innovative ideas- Renewing the mind. By transformation of our minds to the King's big Idea (Did you know that, in the Greek concept of "WORD" expression of thoughts or an Idea or express Idea comes from the word *"LOGOS"*, which means express Idea).

Learning new values must come first from hearing and continuous hearing of right idea (LOGOS). Idea is more powerful because it can change everything. To influence society, we must start with innovative ideas, ideas that will build encourage, motivate, transform, and add value to our fellow human (dignity), only new values will replace old values.

Our Royal values that we learned from the King itself, the benefactors of this will be the next generation of our society and the world. Unlearning old ways and learning royal ideas, ideas which build our personal identity, families, society, rulers, and governments, ideas that will impact and influence established on the royal values and principle of the Kingdom of Heaven, announced by our beloved King Eshua Meshika (King Jesus of Nazareth the Christus).

REASON -9

Right Values empower us to Engage!

"It's not enough to know; one should also use. It's not enough to want – one should also act."

- Johann Wolfgang von Goethe

My wife says – believe in your product

My wife Susan is a business-type woman. She has the audacity mutually with PMA (positive mental attitude) mindset, which she can sell anything she had. No amount of product is impossible for her, in my exaggeration; So, I asked her one time, "Honey, how can I become a confident person in the business world? Where I can sell anything to a specific customer?", she replied and smiled, "Believe" first in yourself that this, your product is proven effective by using it personally. Whether the customer's neither rejects your product nor won't listen to your talk, it doesn't matter; you have to believe it first in yourself that your product is self-tested and proven effective in your life. Therefore, I realized that, in order to engage your customer, first you need to believe if for yourself, that your product is valuable, and worthy to share, promote, and sell it to others, even if others won't believe you or they have their own opinion over your product, it doesn't matter at all, what you believe in your product is the most important thing you ever had.

I learned a universal principle in life, "What you believe is true for you in life, is what you value" means that, If I have a strong esteem self-value, self-worth, and clear self-Identity, therefore, I can engage

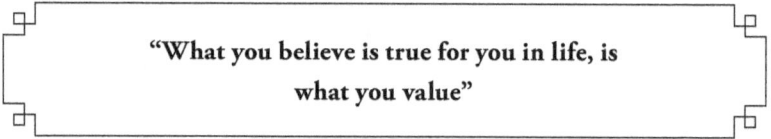

"What you believe is true for you in life, is what you value"

confidently to other people without fear of their rejection and stay humble from their praise.

Clear self-values manifest itself, it creates a sense of deep passion to engage your world or system of influence by means of serving your gift to the world. That's why, in the world of employment – knowing your self-value means that you are believing in yourself that You are significant to the job assignment, that you are engaging people from any department of your organization, to serve them with and for a purpose to deliver your gift to solve a need in this world.

Right values determine your passion

Right values determine your passion, "Why I am doing this? Question of activity; what is passion? Passion is a deep desire in our heart that gives us the will power to do a thing despite of hard work and sacrifice. It is a craving – you are compelled to do it even without partner, you are still decided to pursue it, that's passion.

Passion is a deep resolution and motivation that helps you rise above your daily routine. Passion is a source of energy, values provide a sense of passion because your values are the source of your purpose and therefore, you prioritize your time, talent, and your resources.

Why engage? Who will engage? Our values will dictate why and who will we engage. According to the recent studies conducted by Gallup:

Studies conducted by Dale Carnegie Institute, shows that most of employees, who are actively participated in their company organization are those "feeling valued", which is the sum of all positive feelings that are necessary to generate engagement. Employees value are so important that companies with engage employees outperformed those without by up to 202% (Gallup), four keys of values that leads to employee's engagement – These are enthusiasm, inspired, empowered, and confident. 95% of employees that feel at least 3 of the key positive emotions are engage.

Value is the common key denominator in engaging employees. It produces confident which eventually produce enthusiasm and later inspired and empowered people to do impossible things. Values creates your passion, it fuels our sense of purpose which will ignite you to push even through hard times.

Every value has a result of sense of significance; value generated itself – a sense of importance which will produce confidence to engage another person, family, society, rulers, and governments. Value is the key to secret of wealth. *Excerpt from Dr. Myles Munroe: "Don't pursue success; pursue to become a person of value".*

Why Value? value attracts wealth, it attracts resources, thus in life, the key to engaging people is to have clear self-value(s), generated by our personal purpose, which will fuel our passion, motivated by our sense of vision.

In Kingdom values, the perspective of King's original intention, or his original reason, why he manufactured (create) his own product in his image, nature, and character, is that, He wants to influence the physical earth with his personal values, morals, lifestyle, and culture from the unseen world to the visible world, in which he wants to fill also the earth with his glory (glory in Hebrew concept means "full-weight of his true nature or culture).

The palmist wrote: *"For the earth shall be filled with the knowledge of the glory (culture) of the Lord, as the waters cover the sea."* (See book Habakkuk chapter II, article XIV, KJV).

and

"For the kingdom is the LORD's: and he is the governor among the nations." (See book Psalm chapter XXII, article XXVIII, KJV).

Lost Self-Identity and purpose

Now as one of the biggest problem of human – The Lost and separate from the Kingdom values of our Righteous King because of an act by our ancient ancestor. The first man named *ADAM in Hebrew which mean "dark-earth"*, in his one single act, he caused the entire human generation in his loins (his seed) to declared independent from the King of Kings influence and his Great Source. And therefore, He lost (ADAM) lost the management contract of dominating the world (system of Influence) – The Kingdom dominion of "KOSMOS" (the people inside the system and including the system itself), and also (ADAM) lost his "Kingdom image" – His Royal Sonship (his true nature, character, and his primary function).

After many epochs and millennia, human being was fallen with deep lost contact to the Right Source, they've tried to live in their own might independently and their human wisdom, apart from governing influence of the governor's kingdom country of Heaven (The Governor of the Kingdom of Heaven on earth is the Holy Spirit). Despised and break relationship from our parent-country "Heaven", we've lost our Self-Image, our true Self-Identity in the process, and our pre-destined assignment to rule this earth.

The church (church in Greek word is "ekklesia" which means Royal cabinet or department on earth representing the government of the Kingdom of Heaven on Earth), the universal church as a group, lost the message of our King, replaced by their own religion institutions and rituals or tradition, thus we are totally independent, out-of-disposition and oppressed by a lie coming from the prince of this world, the unemployed cherub, that, we are relegated to be slaves, poor, and lived abusively without purpose and meaning in our lives. Everyone is busy paying their own bills, mortgage, and die. What kind of a depressing state of our human-spirit. Men produce a religion to answer these five questions of the human heart, in trying to find our meaning and purpose in this temporal, physical life.

Five Question of the Human heart that needs to be deal and answer:

1. **Who Am I?** The question of our true-Identity and finding your self-value. Most of the 7.3 billion people around the world doesn't know exactly their identity, worst they believe a lie that, self-Image is what the world tells us. Their self-Image is connected only to the physical earth.

    The world system in which – is design to devalue and destroy our true-self by many distractions in life (i.e. addiction to substance, sexual immorality, politics without principle, business without morality, science without humanity, wealth without work, Pleasure without conscience, knowledge without character, and worship without sacrifice, etc.) and the world system will never help you, it will discourage you in finding your inner self-Identity.

    That's why, many countries today have a high-crime-rate, because people don't know their true self-Identity, So, they steal other people's clothes, shoes, even image, etc. just to exchanged their lost self-image, some join gangs and fraternities; in order to have identity, others tried to wear fashion so that, they can fill the emptiness, the loss of their self-image, with the value of the things in this world. Other, join in a club; wasting money and time, spending foolishly their precious life, receiving only what they've hunger deep inside, the void, meaninglessness life of Who I am.

2. **Where did I come from?** The question of our Heritage – where did our beginning start. Many people, if they were asked, where did they come from? They will say 100%, where they were born from, their native place, their ethnic heritage. But, the reality is quitely sad, our ethnic history was so muddled that you can never be sure, who's, who you parents, grand-parents, were and your ancestor comes from. Maybe you will be shock, if you will find that in your father's lineage, you'll find – Your mother is white, and your father is black or vice-versa, or your grand-father is Chinese while your grandmother is Filipino, thus in every ethnic background was mixed, and all the nations in the world are totally confused from their own True Identity. So far as to say, even if, your' ancestor is quite clear and all their names were written in your family tree, your grand-grand-grand-parents were also confused as to the same degree as with you, Thus, if we trace-back, looking for our ethnic backgrounds, you will be loss. If you are wondering, how to find your true original heritage, you must not stop looking horizontally but try to looked-up transcendentally beyond our physical world and looked for an evidence for the True Source which can't be limit by time, space, and matter. Unless, you find out that, if you're Source is from another world, your values will also come from that world. That World - is unlimited and eternal source of your great inheritance.

3. **Why I was here?** The question of purpose. Why? Unless we have the answer from one of the two previous, we can't find an answer to this metaphysical question. A question of significance to my personal existence. Some people try to avoid this question by doing their own practical deeds pragmatic approach. It can be religion or any humanistic movement, anything that with relates to your accomplishments or your personal practical work. Some tried to find meaning by their

78

own human philosophy through thinking. They say that if you follow certain right thoughts, your life will follow also, maybe others persuade you to try yoga or other meditation of something i.e. empty your mind movement, jut to know your ultimate purpose in the universe.

Others may find their own purpose through their own feelings, you may find this book that I am belong to this 3rd category because most of my personal stories are written in this book, So, you may add me in this category, in finding your own purpose. By the way, if you are looking for your own purpose through your own subjective feelings, you may not also comfortable because most of us had a bad experience which produces bad feelings toward yourself or to others. That may hinder you to pursue your ultimate grand purpose in life. So, how will I find my purpose and meaning in this life?

My personal subjective answer to that metaphysical question will be. If you've noticed my example, I told you above mention that others find their purpose through right doing (pragmatism), others through right thinking (philosophy), and others in right feelings (existentialism), and some they mixed these three methods. They say if your breath properly, and meditate every day, emptying your mind, then you'll find the ultimate purpose in life, what can I only say is – let's go back to our home, Why? In your house, there you'll find many devices, gadgets, equipment's or tools made by a manufacturer. What do I mean? Every manufacturer makes a product by its purpose, before a product goes into release in the market. The manufacturer already finished its purpose before making the product and later mass-produces it.

Purpose comes from the mind of maker/designer/manufacturer. It doesn't come from the opinion of any costumers, distributer, retailer, or any unauthorized dealers. Purpose shall be and only exclusive come from the mind of manufacturer. Only the maker's mind reveals his thoughts, why you were design before assign in this world.

Therefore, Purpose doesn't come from any of the three methods of right doing, right thinking, and right feelings, even if you mixed these three methods or some part of it. **"Meaning and purpose comes from a Person's Mind".** If you want to know the exact meaning of my book, you need to find me "author" of this book, and some of the details of my mind, I already write it in this book to reveal my thoughts toward you, Also, if you want to know your grand-purpose in life you must come back to the mind of your manufacturer which is ELOHIM INC, Our CEO is our Abba, Our Source, Our Father and his Son, Eshua (Jesus) is our right-manager. Only in him the grand-author, grand-manufacturer only you can find your true purpose in life.

4. **What is my true ability?** The question of potential. What is my capacity and my gift to influence the world. Is there any significant of my life in relation to this world of humanity? In my previous chapters, I talked about, Purpose determines your ability. I believe, If He designs – He assign. If He calls for – then He provides for. If He intent – He invent. If He made you then He equips you, whatever the purpose of the product, its capacities and function are already built-in the products. Like your cellular phone; before the manufacturer release it in the market, He designs it to function by/to receive call, and make a call, and the phone does not doubt in his capacity to accept/make a phone call because that is why its purpose has made, it's built-in to the product itself. Whatever the makers-mind or what we called "manufacturer's manual" to read it for yourself, what functions he built-inside of you and to know your ultimate hidden potential trap inside of you. "come and see" his manual for your life. He already reveals his Idea (LOGOS) in his book towards your purpose and ability.

5. **Where is my destination?** The question of destiny, where shall I go? Is there any future for me? A Vision for my personal life. According to the manual, I know what will be my sense of destination. Your vision and destination isn't buying a house beside the lake, million dollars inside the bank, many awards, accolades, trophies to be receive, or position and power, all of these latter are called "ambition" and not "vision". Vision is for other people, others will be the beneficiaries of your true purpose and meaning in life and not by you.

Vision helps others and not oppressed people, it inspired them and not manipulating them for your own benefit, it builds-up, it edifies one another, it encourages, it adds value to others, it never suppresses people but release them to be themselves, unique, being original according to the mind of the maker. All kinds of religion and human philosophies have tries to answer this question, to deal this kind metaphysical question; only the manufacturer's mind can only suffice the person destiny for him.

Summary of the five questions

All of these five (5) questions can be summarized into:

1. Question of Identity
2. Question of Source
3. Question of Purpose
4. Question of Significance
5. Question of Destiny

Only the Maker's (manufacturer's) mind knows the answered for all of these questions, and that's why, we need personally to come back to him, not for any religious emotional experience, rituals, and traditions, but, you want to seek him because You need to find the answers, ONLY in Him and no one else can provide you except him, the Alpha and the Omega! The chief Cornerstone of our human Identity and Purpose.

Seven Valuables of Self-Keys in finding His (Our King) Purpose in your life:

1. **What is your deepest desire?** This is a desire that never stops recurring in your life, it is more than death, and this desire can't stop by fear of losing your life, for the sake of your personal significance in life.

2. **What is your passion born out of your convictions?** These convictions came from your belief, it is where your source of motivation and meaning to your existence. Passion is greater than death, it fuels you to achieve no matter what's the cost of sacrifice.

3. **What makes you angry?** This idea of being angry, or hate, is tied-up to the concept of purpose due to numerous problems by being born to solve and correct what's necessary for completing your assignment here on earth. i.e. Oppression, poverty human-devaluation, and many other negative symptoms of our human fallen-nature.

4. **What are your recurring dreams for humanity?** These dreams are not for personal benefits but for humanity cause or sake. Ambition is for yourself only, i.e. A million dollar in the account, or buy house beside the lake, own a business, etc. while vision is for the other to benefit using your life for their benefits. It is a dream for alleviating, prevent, preserve, protect, and promote human-value and dignity to the next generation and maintain it.

5. **What brings you the greatest return of fulfillment?** It's the question of personal satisfaction or personal meaning in our life. It is well said by one of the Philosopher in the times of Tiberius Caesar says, "It is better to give than receive", it is when our gift is used to serve to the world needs and

expecting nothing in return then it would generate meaning and deeper satisfaction in our human spirit.

6. **What can you do forever, even if, there's no monetary compensation?** In our modern times, most people are doing their own thing for the purpose of self-benefiting for money. Many students around the world just studying just to look for a better, secured, paying-job, high-salary, pay-bills & mortgage, be merry and later die. This question deals with our self-motivation and finding what is your passion is, even if, there's no (ROI) Return of Investments, but you still decide to self-sacrifice and paid it, for the benefit of others.

7. **What would you become rather than doing?** Most people when they ask, "Who are you?" they've respond in what they are doing, usually their job, career, or position in the corporate world. But, few people understand that who you are and what's your work are totally different entity. Work means **"to become"** or **"manifest your true self"**. It is tied-up to the Identity of a person and not on what he/she is doing, Work "to become" in the old literature of Hebrew means **"ergon" means Work.**

It means you are assign because you are design by the author itself. It is different from your job, job is temporary, work is permanent, job is related to your skills, and work is related to your gift/inborn talents.

Job is what they paid you to do, work is something you are born to do, work is simply our purpose, the original intention, why we are here on the planet earth, it is the reason why I was born, it is the intention before the invention. Becoming begins with self-discovery of your true deep purpose and deciding to become yourself and manifesting it and decide to serve it to the world.

Summary of seven (7) valuable of self-keys:

Write down all of your answers in your diary, or any form of storage (digital is convenient) because you will need to read I again and again. No one knows your pre-destines purpose, even your parents, teachers, pastors, priest, imam, cardinal, coach, supervisor, and even your wife/husband. ONLY the words and the voice of the manufacturer and his manual will only reveal who you are, and what you are born to do, that's why, in knowing our King of Kings is not religion experience, it's a personal relationship between you and your manufacturer, if you are really interested in with your deep-calling purpose in life. You must come back to him – Our King and Lord of Lords, which his name is King Eshua (Jesus) the Meshika (Messiah).

> "Seek Him – His purpose for you is already
> been written in his manual, all you need is Come
> and see"

Three (3) values of stages– From King's Purpose for your life:

1. **You must Arise (Self-discovery)** – No one or any other people can say to you or show to you about your true purpose in life, once the Maker's mind reveals/unveils/shows it to you, you must arise from your past-identity by taking the new Identity. Decide it for yourself; accept it, what He intends for you, between you and your Manufacturer only, in my personal case, once I discovered my true purpose in life through my Chief Cornerstone – Eshua (Jesus). I write it on a piece of paper, and rewrite it on a white-board; I need to see it every day to remind me, what is the cause of my human existence as per my manufacturers' manual, it takes only a DECISION then PURSUE it, his Purpose for your life with all of your heart, mind, soul, and strength. Once you discovered your purpose, you are a different man/

woman because you will become your original self (product) without any imitation or competition or comparing to other products.

2. **You must Go (Self-Awareness)** – After personal decision, you must act in your own small way to pursue your purpose. You will also be aware that not everyone will be comfortable or agree, in what you will become doing in the next few days, months, or years, because they will be surprised in your own attitude and your actions, than, what you are now is, very different from their own opinion to you. Not everyone will agree to, support you, encourage you, or help you in pursuing your unique God-ultimate purpose, sometimes (if not common) many will turn-back on you, but despite of that, it doesn't matter anymore, as long as you are true to yourself and you are clear to what is the Mind of our Maker's reveals to you. Take note – find a mentor similar in your true purpose (not exactly the same) that can fertilize your purpose and not the ones who will pollute your God-given-vision, remember choose your mentor based on your destination.

3. **You must Become (Self-Manifestation)** – As I walked now, first from accepting the Maker's mind original intention for my own existence, second from taking decision and taking small action, next is; to become yourself by manifesting it. Attitude plus Ability equals success (according to one's unique purpose and cause and not subject to anyone's opinion about you. Self-Manifestation requires effort and more effort and responsibility than your formerly beliefs. It requires his empowerment; his purpose for your life will be the driving factors in your whole entire life.

Your habit, diet, interest, friends, is totally-focused on one thing which is your ultimate-purpose in life. Your life will be now simplified and eliminated by all the distraction. it will always be self-fulfilled, even-if, you will find yourself inside the storm, wind, or any challenges-in-life, you will become storm-proof, wind-shield, and overcomer in this life.

Summary of Three (3) values of stages from Knowing Your Purpose:

Before these ends; please take note that, in all of these mentions above, it requires right environment, right-information idea (logos), right-mentor, external source (which means the Manufacturer) and time.

In the same analogy - In the **Principle of Seed**: Imagine you are the seed; the seed before it manifests to become a tree (his vision/destination), his purpose is to become that vision. The seed must be buried inside the soil which means you need the right environment, because not all environments will edify you, only inside the right-soil. Next, you need water which is the right-information which always come inside the manual of the manufacturer and not to anyone's idea/opinion of you. Next, you need fertilizer in order to grow and become strong, which means you need a person or group of persons which is always aligned according to your own destination. Not everyone is qualifying to help you, to accomplish and finish your destiny, thus chose your mentor according to your destination.

Next, the seed needs sun-light which mean you need the external input from the Grand-author, or the Manufacturer itself, which creates you and your purpose for his name sake. You need daily relationship with Eshua (Jesus) through his powerful announcement, ideas, and teaching about the Kingdom of God and lastly, the seed requires time; the seed needs ample time before it takes and manifests its vision – To Become Tree. It takes patience with time, learn from every season of life, catch every season, adapt to your environment, but not become your environment.

In his proper and appointed time, you will become Tree (proper season) then, the last stages will be being – Bearing fruit. This fruit will serve others, this is the ultimate (His) purpose for us is to bear fruit and serve it to the world and for promotion, up-holding, advancement, and securing the humanity sake, means your fruit will benefit others more than you, that's why, you will become valuable to the world. Value attracts success. In rapid, brief, recall above-mention:

Seed needs – Right environment (soil), Right information (water), Right mentor (fertilizer), Sun-light (King Eshua teaching about the Kingdom of God, and lastly, it needs Time (season).

Knowing his purpose; knows your true Image and your unique assignment to this world.

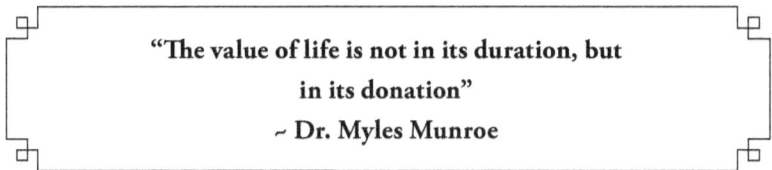

"The value of life is not in its duration, but in its donation"

~ Dr. Myles Munroe

Chapter Three in a Nutshell

The Power of Kingdom values

A. Right Values interprets vision
1. Right values determine your destiny.
2. What you believed – you value.
3. What you understand is what you respond.
4. Worthy is the measure of items express in value.
5. The worth of a product depends on the integrity of the Manufacturer to protect its vision and purpose.
6. You give worth to what you value.
7. Vision is the source of our determination. It fuels our passion. It gives self-discipline and it determines our destiny.

B. Right Values supports acceptance
1. Image comes from your Source. (*Kingdom of Heaven* as source determines my personal image).
2. Values come from Image.
3. Values reflect the Identity of its source.

C. Right Values enables continuous learning
   1. Right learning that leads to life – start with the foundation "Respect of the Lord" (Lord Means A Mighty owner/Master).
   2. Right values determine your ability.
   3. Ability is according to his (King) purpose and function specifically for you – "What he assigns, he designs"
   4. Right values bring right investment.
   5. Source determines the ability of the thing itself.
   6. Ability determines our purpose in life – "What he calls for, he provides for".
   7. The Fear (respect) of the Lord is the beginning of Wisdom.

D. Right Values purge old habits to Unlearn
   1. Right values affect our action, and constant action, affects our habit.
   2. Right values determine your purpose.

E. Right Values empowers us to Engage
   1. What you believe is true for you in life, is what you value.
   2. Right values determine your purpose.
   3. Right values are the common key denominator in keys of Engaging.
   4. Right values result from the sense of Significance.
   5. Human heart needs to deal and answer the Question of: self-Identity, Source, Purpose, Potential, and Destiny.
   6. Three values of stages from knowing your Purpose – Self-discovery, Self-Awareness, and Self-Manifestation.
   7. Engaging starts from discovering self-purpose and working it out to manifest your true nature and decide to serve your gift (fruit) to the world.

GLOSSARY

Behavior - the way we act or conduct ourselves, esp. towards others.

Commodity – the product made by the manufacturer which has intrinsically valuable and worth.

Conviction – strong belief on the base of truth or eternal principle built-in nature and super-nature or above-nature ("spirit" – literally mean "from above").

Image – It means same degree in nature, character (from characteristics) and also, make by the manufacturer to certify that the product released was tested and approved by the manufacturer's standards. Thus, the Manufacturer built into product laws in which it needs to operate by and fulfill its design-function and ultimately its purpose.

Keys – are simply built-in principle in this world made by the manufacturers to its own deem product. It's the symbol of authority given by the King itself, to unlock/lock things on earth by using simple profound keys (principles or truth).

King – one who rules a country by birth, has the right to sovereign, rulership, kingship, or the title given to a Lord sustaining a land called his dominion (his territory), exercising his own personal will, intention, desire, moral standards, and his personal values. *("Malik-Arabic", "Melekh-Hebrew")*

Kingdom – is a placed ruled by a King, located from a distant parent-country and aims to colonize other place (called colony) for the expansion of the Kingdom and King's territory, which is called his Domain; Exercising his dominion, rulership, and kingship. King's motivation is to influence the colony with his personal will (purpose) that will live a mark, imprint, an inspiration, and an impact of his glory (the word glory in Hebrew can be mean "true full-weight of nature" from the word "kabod) to the colony itself, leaving his lifestyle, culture, moral standards, and his personal values. *("Malakūt-Arabic, Malkhūt-Hebrew")*

Lord – Mighty Owner or Master, which has the legal-authority to own a thing by his ownership rights. *("Rabba-Arabic, "Ado nay-Hebrew")*

Manual – The mind of the manufacturer in which, all the basic principles or Timeless truth are built-in inside the product and written to inform us the customer (people) about his product (life-purpose). It simply gives us knowledge about his mind pertaining to his own product.

Manufacturer – The one who creates, design, and sustain the world "kosmos".

Power – is our capacity or ability of our deep, hidden, true, potential based on our received purpose from the King; it is connected to our true design and how we are wired to fulfilled the assignment, we are here purposely on earth. Power simply the manifestation of our belief, attitude, and conviction based on the Word of Author/Manufacturer's manual.

Principle – Basic eternal truth which is established and built-in inside the creation (seen/unseen) world by the manufacturer's Idea. Can be natural such as gravity, magnetism, etc. and can be supernatural such as but not limited to forgiveness.

Priority – First thing first, the ordered or rank of important items which is usually consist of only two or three items in ordered.

Thus, priorities are most valuable things in life that can't neglect and must be established. it makes anything simplified.

Rarity – The product is so rare that the value becomes high and higher to a certain type of commodity such as gold or silver or petrol.

Value (Values) – principles that we value and are necessary for us to function by and fulfill our higher purpose, or inner convictions of what we believe, the Truth. It influences our decision, it comes from passion, which fuels by vision, produce by purpose, convicted by sense of truth. Our value is in the essence of our human dignity (dignity in Latin means worth) and not by our own achievements, memorial plaques, medals, ribbon, or any accolades; human value (life) comes from the Image of our Source/Manufacturer. *("Alqayima-Arabic, erekh-Hebrew")*

Vision – The picture of your purpose, the future address of your purpose, it operates on your belief and not by your own sight (eyes).

Worthy – Is the measure of items express in value, determines how much you pay for it.

SYNOPSIS

"**R**ediscover your unique Timeless value" talks about the keys (timeless principles) built-in through the message of our King Eshua (Jesus) long time ago, about his government country "the Kingdom of Heaven". Rediscovering his timeless message means we need to go back again from time and study and learn from his timeless teaching and realign ourselves through the value of his message.

In this book, are the Nine (9) reasons, why, "Right-values specifically "Kingdom values" gives us purpose and meaning in our existential life.

➢ Reason no.1 - Right values drives right behavior
➢ Reason no.2 - Right values gives right destination
➢ Reason no.3 – Right values correct priorities and organize
➢ Reason no.4 – Right values inspires dedication
➢ Reason no.5 – Right values interprets vision
➢ Reason no.6 – Right values support acceptance
➢ Reason no.7 – Right values enables continuous learning
➢ Reason no.8 – Right values purge old habits to Unlearn

➢ Reason no.9 – Right values empower us to Engage

Also, Here, you will find-out the "Purpose, Priority, and the Power of Kingdom values", which empower you - yourself-values concept, and influence your idea of who you are, and what you can do to the world and for the better of humanity. This book helps you find your own unique "timeless value" which will determine your significance and meaning of your life.

This book is also constituted of my personal autobiography stories and the corresponding keys of the Kingdom of God that I've personally understand.

Reading "Rediscover your unique timeless value", then they will:

➢ Understand the purpose, priority, and power of our human values.
➢ Be able to rediscover, what we've lost through many centuries about the teaching values of the Kingdom of God through the person of Eshua (Jesus) the Christ of Nazareth.
➢ Study and learn effective timeless principles from the King's timeless teachings.

Because the book will:

➢ Provide information's on how to discover our unique timeless value.
➢ Outline keys of principles for effective-living according to the manual of the manufacturers about the "Kingdom of God" influence on earth.
➢ Build yourself self-values on Kings timeless concept.

Suggested books:

After reading this book, I humbly personally endorse these following items for your further readings about our values:

1. Kingdom Principles by Dr. Myles Munroe
2. Understanding your Potential by Dr. Myles Munroe
3. Employees engagement "Understanding value" by Dale Carnegie
4. Man's search for Meaning by Dr. Viktor Frankl
5. Rich dad/Poor Dad by Robert Kiyosaki

www.ingramcontent.com/pod-product-compliance
Lightning Source LLC
Chambersburg PA
CBHW020537290526
45786CB00002B/923